Children
Becoming
READERS

How It Happens in the Home

Tom S. Schroeder

ISBN: 979-8-35093-023-8 paperback

ISBN: 979-8-35093-024-5 ebook

This book is dedicated to Steven –who taught me more about reading than all the professors and scholars I have encountered over the years.

CONTENTS

ACKNOWLEDGMENTS

This book is the result of decades of experiences with all kinds of wonderful people who have been part of my own personal and professional life. That life has involved a continuous journey toward understanding and appreciating the amazing phenomenon of children becoming a part of a literate culture. It began with six wonderful years of teaching at Apache Elementary School in Overland Park, Kansas. It took on new direction under the mentorship of Dr. Lee Capps and Dr. Nita Wyatt at the University of Kansas and has been given life by students and colleagues during thirty-six wonderful years at Ball State University.

I especially want to thank Dr. Barbara Weaver Smith, whose encouragement led me to carry this project out, and whose knowledge and outstanding editorial skills have carried me to complete the book and bring it to publication.

Most of all, I want to thank my children—Dana, Steven, and Emily—who lived out my journey before my eyes and allowed me to experience the joy of seeing literacy become a part of life.

INTRODUCTION

"Once you learn to read, you will be forever free."
—Frederick Douglas

Don't we want more than anything for our children to be free? Free to grow, free to do, free to choose, free to be? Reading is a key to all kinds of freedom, and the home can be an important place where that freedom is born and nurtured.

This book is for parents, and also for teachers, grandparents, and friends—for anyone who is anxious to help the children in their life become strong readers. But this is not a "Teach Your Child How to Read" book. It's not a learning-to-read "method" that will suddenly transform your child into a star reader. It doesn't happen that way. Becoming a good reader takes time, direct instruction, and it takes special attention from the adults surrounding a child.

Whether your child is attending school, or you are doing home-schooling, this book is written to help you understand more of what reading is all about and what is happening when children are learning to read. There is so much you can do at home to help your kids become great readers. In fact, your home can be a critical and powerful factor in their reading success.

Assuming they sleep eight hours a day, children spend around 5,780 hours awake in a year. Once they are school age, they will spend about 1,000 of those hours in school, and a small number of those 1,000 hours getting reading instruction. How do they spend those other 4,780 hours? Can some of those hours spent at home and in your community help them become good readers?

I think that's a big YES. And that's what this book is all about.

PART ONE:
WELCOME HOME!

Do you have a child who is in the process of learning to read? Do you wonder (or worry) about how that will happen? Most importantly, do you wonder about how you can have a role to play in this critical part of your child's development? Why is the home so important to children learning to read? And how does the home life of a child contribute to learning to read? In this beginning section of the book, I want you to understand two big ideas about how your home is a critical factor that will influence how your child develops as a reader. So, I welcome you and welcome your home into your child's reading life. Let's get started.

CHAPTER ONE:
MAKING IT HAPPEN –
THE BIG THREE

"The more that you read, the more things you will know. The more that you learn, the more places you'll go."
–Dr. Seuss

Imagine yourself in the middle of a well-equipped and well-stocked kitchen. You have a big collection of beautiful, fresh raw ingredients and a fancy stove and sharp knives and lots of counter space with everything you need to make a perfect meal and enjoy eating it. And you are a very good cook. But … you're not hungry. In fact, you are completely full, and the thought of food doesn't even cross your mind. My guess is that you're not going to take the time and go to the trouble of cooking. There's no point! **It doesn't matter how great the conditions are for you to do something, or how great you are at it, if you see no reason for doing it, you won't do it—especially if it takes some time and effort.**

Now imagine that you are a person who loves to eat—and loves to cook—and you're good at it. You can imagine yourself preparing a scrumptious meal and enjoying it with some friends. And you're hungry! But … you've got no food to prepare and no kitchen to work in. Under those circumstances, you can't prepare a great meal even if you want to. **It doesn't**

matter how motivated you are to do something; if you don't have the <u>opportunity</u> to do it, you won't do it.

OK, one more time, now imagine yourself back in the kitchen. This time you are hungry. You crave a great meal. You are motivated to create something special for you and your friends to enjoy. All the great raw ingredients are there. All the appliances you need are there. You have unlimited time to spend on cooking and enjoying a terrific meal. Only one problem: You don't know how to cook! You don't have a cookbook or a recipe. And even if you did, you probably couldn't follow it because you know nothing about cooking. You think boiled eggs just come that way from certain kinds of chickens. You don't know the first thing about how to turn those raw ingredients into a meal. **It doesn't matter how much you want to do something and how many resources are there to do it. If you don't know <u>how</u> to do it, you won't.**

These three scenarios illustrate "the big three" elements that need to be present for anyone to do anything:

- They need to have a <u>reason</u> to do it.
- They need to have the <u>opportunity</u> to do it.
- They need to have the <u>tools</u> to do it.

This is absolutely true of learning to read. To be successful, our children need to have *reasons* to read, *opportunities* to read, and the *tools* to read. If these three elements are not present in their lives, learning to read will be a struggle. Let's briefly look at these three ideas.

First, what about having a <u>reason</u> to read? Think about it What reasons do our children have to read? In school, the reason is usually that the teacher *tells* the children to read. They are *assigned* the task of reading. They are told what to read and when to read. Of course, having an assignment in school is a legitimate reason to read, but no one ever learns to love reading if they only read when they are told to.

That's where your home life can play a leading role. You can make reading a vital part of your child's life. Take a moment to think about some ways you can give your child reasons to read at home or in your community.

First, there are *practical* reasons for reading, like reading you the recipe while you're cooking, or looking up and reading information about the place you'll be going for vacation, or finding reviews for a new movie, or reading letters or text messages from friends or family.

Then there are *personal* reasons to read, like reading books of their favorite author, or articles about some idea that's close to their heart, or an issue that worries them, or a skill they want to learn. Children need to know that their home is the place where reading is a way to indulge their interests, explore their problems, and pursue their desires.

Second, they have to have the opportunity to read. Here is where your home has a huge role to play. Teachers work hard to find time for children to read in school, but they have lots of required activities to carry out and many subjects to cover. Opportunities to engage in reading are clearly limited in school.

But you can provide almost unlimited opportunities for your children to read. One very important way is just to *make print available*. Why do you pick up that magazine on the table in the doctor's office waiting room? Because it's *there*. The question is, what is there for your child in your home?

We all know that there is huge competition for your child's attention. What is almost always available these days is technology. If an appealing game is instantly available on a cell phone or tablet, and nothing else is around, guess what will capture your child's attention.

Think about what your child is interested in or is passionate about. Are there books and magazines around that speak to his interests and his passions? He won't pick them up if they don't exist!

Making sure that appealing and interesting reading materials are available in your home takes work and time and attention. It could involve visiting libraries and museums and other places that are rich in print materials. And it means taking advantage of opportunities to use technology to find interesting information and to take virtual field trips. But the investment is worth it – not only because it contributes to reading power, but also because it contributes to your child's growth as a person.

In addition to making print available in your home, you can make *time* available, too. Actually, the time is there. Remember all those hours that your child is not in school? The question is, can you help to see that some of those hours are spent in real reading activities?

An effective way to make this happen is to set aside a regular time when adults and children just read. It doesn't need to be long or programmed. Everyone decides what they want to read. You simply set a time for reading. I think you might be surprised at what could happen. Your children get valuable time to practice reading and it could spark some interesting family conversations. If you start this when your child is young, it will be a familiar practice by the time he is a teenager. As you think about it, you will find many other ways to help make time available for reading in your home.

So, as a parent, what happens in your home is crucial for your children to find *reasons* to read and *opportunities* to read in their everyday life. What about the third element of the "big three" —the <u>tools</u> to read? This is clearly where we look to the schools for leadership. Research regarding the science of reading is continuously leading to new insights about how reading should be taught.

Can you as parents and concerned adults help provide your children the skills and competence needed to read effectively? Absolutely! In fact, that's what the rest of this book is all about. As you learn more about what reading is, you will discover that the home is a critical place to help children acquire the tools they need to become powerful and effective readers.

So What?

In this chapter, we've stressed that's it's important to give your children practical and personal *reasons* to read, and to give them *opportunities* to read by making lots of print materials available and making time available for reading. What might this look like in your home?

Look for reasons for your child to read. How about having your child "look up" something for you (on-line, in the newspaper, in a recipe book, etc.) or going through the mail for the day and telling you about what's there for the family. Or write your child a note on a regular basis (like every Friday morning) and put it in a special place where she will always find it. Or give your child something you have read that you think is meaningful and ask his opinion or reaction.

There are endless ways to provide children with reasons to read, but they won't always occur to a child without someone drawing their attention to them. You have to be *intentional*. Take a thoughtful look at what's going on in your home. What are some things that can naturally give your child a reason to engage with print? Go for it.

Likewise, you must be intentional about providing your children opportunities to read at home by making print and time available. Intentionally place interesting reading materials in strategic locations in the house. Set aside a time for yourself to read. Let your child know that he's welcome to join you. Talk about things that your child is interested in and cares about. Find reading materials related to her passions and have them available. When you're out and about, pick up flyers and notices from merchants and community agencies. Ask your child about what they say. Ask your child what signs are saying as you are out in the car. Again, there are endless opportunities for children to engage with print Be intentional. Take advantage of them.

No doubt the most important thing you can do with your child is reading <u>to</u> him and reading <u>with</u> him. Reading to a child from the very beginning provides a foundation for making literacy a vital part of his life. It provides not only a reason and opportunity for reading, but also develops fundamental patterns that underlie the development of the tools of reading.

What's Next?

So that is the first big idea about learning to read. For reading to happen, there needs to be a *reason* to read, *opportunity* to read, and the *tools* to read. We have spent some time in this chapter thinking about providing reasons and opportunities for reading in the home. In the next chapter, we'll discuss the fundamental thing that <u>you</u> as a parent need in order to provide your child these tools of reading.

Finally, reading to your child introduces her to the joy of reading and the value of reading. It connects her to all kinds of real and imaginary characters who introduce her to hilarious situations and touching relationships. It puts her in touch with other children in stories who demonstrate and model how life works for them and helps her navigate her own thoughts about her life. In short, reading to your child can provide a whole world of experiences that can't be gained any other way, and that will be with her forever.

CHAPTER TWO:
DO THE RIGHT THING

"Children are made readers on the laps of their parents."
—Emilie Buchwald

One day a man needed to get a heavy stump onto the bed of his pickup truck. It looked like a pretty straightforward task. He knew he was strong enough to do it, and it was something that really needed to be done. So, after a deep breath, he approached the stump, bent over, got a grip, and began to lift. Suddenly, the neighborhood echoed with unpleasant sounds and unexpected vocabulary as the man dropped the stump, grabbed his back in pain, and simultaneously began jumping around in the hope that this would relieve the pain in the toes on which the stump had landed.

Intrigued and a little concerned by the noises he had heard, a neighbor came quickly and discovered what had happened. After a brief conversation, the neighbor, who was of the same age and physical build, volunteered to help. He squatted on his haunches, wrapped his arms around the stump, leaned slightly backward, and slowly stood up. He then pivoted by moving his feet in short little steps and deposited the stump on the pickup bed while his friend stared at him in disbelief.

Why tell you this story? Here's a hint—that neighbor is a physical therapist. He has spent his whole career learning about how the human body works. He spends every day helping patients to make the best use of their muscles and bones. He knew from his training what muscles were larger and stronger and how they worked together. He knew where muscles and joints could handle stress and where they couldn't. In other words, he had a real understanding of how the body works. As a result, he simply did the right thing needed to lift the heavy stump.

The point is simple: If you <u>understand</u> something, you will naturally be able to see ways you can help make it happen. When you understand how something works, you will tend to do the right thing, just as the second neighbor "did the right thing."

So, this is a key for parents and other important adults to help children become good readers: *understand the reading process.* This is a key point of this book. When you understand what is happening when children are learning to read, you will naturally *do the right thing.* It doesn't take a new set of reading books, or a new on-line program, or hiring a special tutor. What it takes is adults who understand what reading all is about and who make good choices for their children based on that understanding.

My purpose in writing this book is to help you understand what reading is all about so you can help your child become a good reader. A big goal, but worth the effort and very satisfying.

Do you remember how you learned to read? Maybe you recall what your "reading book" was like, or the worksheets you had to do, or being embarrassed when you had to read out loud in front of the other kids. But none of that explains how you became a reader. Do you know what you are actually *doing* when you read? Could you explain the processes you are going through right now as you read?

Probably not. And that's OK. However, as you go through this book, I think you will discover that the reading process is fascinating. And, as you understand it increasingly, you begin to have a deeper appreciation for what is happening with your children as they are learning to read. I hope that when you have finished this book, you will have a new point of view about "the reading process"—how it happens, how it develops, and **how you can promote it in your children**.

So What?

It's important for adults in a child's life to understand the reading process, because—just like the physical therapist—if we understand what's happening as children are learning to read, we will naturally "do the right thing" in being helpful to them.

Learning to read is the result of many common factors, and the more these factors are present in a child's life the more likely the child will become a good reader. How well a child learns to read doesn't only depend on how good his school is, or by what reading method she is taught, or even the quality of her teachers. All these things play a role, and we want them to be the best possible. Yet, your child's reading ability ultimately also depends on the culture of literacy that surrounds him as he grows up. And that depends on how well the adults in your child's home understand the reading process.

What's Next?

In this chapter, we have explored the second big idea that forms the foundation of helping your child to become a reader, and that is understanding the process of reading. In Part Two, we'll take a look at what reading is all about. Let's go!

PART TWO:
WHERE TO START

In Part One, my goal was to introduce two important ideas. The first is that the home has a critical role to play in reading development by providing reasons to read, opportunities to read, and tools needed to read. The second is to show that you as a parent will make good choices if you understand what reading is all about. In Part Two, you will get a clear picture of exactly what is happening when someone is reading. We will then describe how what happens in the home makes reading possible. When you are finished with this section, you will understand the two essential foundations of reading, and how you as a parent are critical in building these two foundations for reading with your children.

CHAPTER THREE:
WHAT IS READING?

"Books are a uniquely portable magic."
–Stephen King

This is a book about reading. If we are going to do the right thing to help our children become good readers, we better understand what it is we are asking them to do. So, what is reading anyway? Let's examine that question.

Here's an experiment you might want to do. Think how you would answer this question: "What is reading?" You might want to ask five or six others – including children. Ask them to tell you what reading is. What definitions of reading do they come up with?

You will probably get some responses about how wonderful reading is or how important reading is in their life (or how they don't like reading!). But my guess is that the answers may be something like this:

"Reading is figuring out how to pronounce the words on the page so that you can get meaning from the print."

Think about it. Isn't this the way most people think about what reading is? You look at the printed words and figure out what the words say. Then, those words will reveal the meaning that the writer intended. I'm guessing that this description is the way many people think of reading both in school and at home.

Though it *sounds* reasonable and accurate, it's not exactly what is happening. In fact, in some ways this is really the *opposite* of what is happening when people read.

"What?" you ask. "Really?" Yep. Stay with me.

Two basic ideas are involved in this definition of reading. The first idea is "figuring out how to pronounce the words" and the second idea is "getting meaning from print." I want to briefly explore each of these ideas with you.

Figuring out how to pronounce the words.

Let me ask you a question. How do you know how to pronounce the words you are reading right now? Are you figuring out how to say the words from reading them on the page? I'm pretty sure the answer is "no." Well then, how then *do* you figure out how to say all those words

Actually, that's kind of a trick question, because the truth is, you *already know how to say* the words you read. Think about it. Nearly all of the words you find on a page you have learned how to say as part of learning your first language. You learned without being taught and without really paying attention. From the moment you began to talk somewhere in your first year, you added word after word to your listening and speaking vocabulary very fast. By the time you were two, you could probably say and understand more than a thousand words. And the number kept growing.

Think about the things you read—text messages, magazines, Facebook posts, bills, recipes, books. Nearly every word you see is one you *already know how to say.* Once in a while, you may come across a word that you've never heard before and don't know how to say. When that happens, it's probably someone's name (like Zbigniew Brzezinski), or a scientific term (like Tetraflurohydrazine), or a foreign word (like faux pas). But mostly, you *already know* how to say the words you read, don't you?

Think about it. As you are reading this book right now, how many words have you come across that you didn't already know how to pronounce (except perhaps three in the previous paragraph)? My guess is—none.

Bottom line: We don't learn how to pronounce words by reading them. We already know how to pronounce them. Reading is actually the act of recognizing words in print **that you already know how to pronounce.**

Let's illustrate this idea this way: Suppose a child is reading a book and he comes across the word "tractor." And suppose that this child has grown up on a farm. Does he need to learn how to pronounce "tractor"? Not a chance. He's heard that word and probably said that word hundreds or thousands of times. He didn't learn it from sounding it out while reading. He doesn't need to stop and think about it. It's a part of him. He *knows* how to pronounce that word!

Look at it another way. When you sit down and read a book to your toddler, you fully expect that she knows what you are saying, don't you? You read a book that uses words she *already knows*—words that she has heard many times and that she probably uses herself. That's why she can understand and enjoy the book you are reading to her. Let's face it, if you are reading your child a book with words she has never heard that she cannot understand, I think you may have the wrong book! She's not going to like that book very much! In fact, it would be nonsense.

Maybe you're wondering, "Well, what about words I see in print that I don't already know—words that I've never heard before and I don't know how to say?" That's a great question, and I will explain that point a little later. But for now, here's the first key point: *Reading is nearly always a matter of recognizing printed words that are already familiar in speech and hearing.*

Getting meaning

Now let's look at the second part of our definition of reading, the idea of "getting meaning from print." Just like the notion of pronouncing words, that's not exactly what is happening in reading. In fact, we don't get meaning from print because there is *no meaning* at all on a printed page. (There is only ink.) So, where does the meaning come from?

Well, that's a really important question, and how you answer that question is very important for how you help your children to be successful readers!

Think again of the child who runs across the word "tractor" in the book he is reading. Remember that he is growing up on a working farm. He has seen tractors, heard tractors, smelled tractors, touched tractors, ridden on tractors, and helped his dad drive a tractor. When he recognizes the word "tractor" he immediately *knows* what that word means in a very deep way. He doesn't figure out what that word means from reading it. The meaning of that word is in him. It's a part of his experience.

Now suppose another child sees that same word "tractor" while reading that book. But this child is growing up in the city and has no idea about farming. He's never been on a farm. He has never seen a tractor, never heard the word, and knows nothing about machines that work in fields. Does he get the meaning of that word from reading it on a page? Of course not. He might get some clues from pictures or other words on the page, but real meaning for him must come from somewhere else.

So, where does meaning come from? Meaning comes from *experience*. In fact, instead of saying that reading is getting meaning from print, it is more accurate to say that *reading is taking meaning to print*. This is an important point. *Meaning comes from the reader, not the book.* The words on the page can only call up meanings that the reader already has through experience. *Words are labels for experiences.* Your child is a bundle of meanings! And those meanings have come from the experiences that your child has had.

In Chapter One, I said that children need *reasons* to read, *opportunities* to read and the *tools* to read. In this chapter, you have learned that having lots of rich **experiences** and engaging in continuous **language** about those experiences are the two most important tools your children need to be equipped with if they are to become effective and involved readers. And where is the most important place where children can learn lots of words and will have lots of rich experiences? You got it! It's in the home, and you are the best ones to supply them to your children.

So What?

Was the explanation of reading in this chapter new to you? Did you think of reading this way? Does it make sense to you? What insights did you gain? What questions came to your mind? You might find it fun and interesting to explore these ideas with your own children. Ask your child what he thinks reading is, or how she knows what the words are on the page, or how she decided what a given reading passage means. Talking with your children about what *they* think reading is all about might give you some new and interesting insights about their reading.

What's Next?

In this chapter, we have seen that there are two basic foundations that children need in order to become good readers – a powerful command of *language*, and a rich background of *meaningful experiences*. So where do our children get these foundations? And how do we as parents make sure that these foundations are a solid as possible in our children? That's what we'll explore in the next three chapters.

CHAPTER FOUR:
WHERE DOES READING COME FROM?

"A book is a gift you can open over and over again."

–Garrison Keillor

In our last chapter, we learned that when children read, they are (1) recognizing printed words that they probably already know how to pronounce, and (2) giving those words meanings that have come from their past experiences. That's what reading involves.

So, here's the question: How do our children get to the point that they can do all this stuff we've been talking about? How is it that they know all these words and have all these meanings to bring to print? How does this happen? Where do these skills and abilities come from? It's happening on your watch, but you may have never taken the time to think about it. That's what we'll do in this chapter.

Think about this: children aren't born speaking their language. They also are not born with ideas and concepts about the world around them. Beginning at birth, your child begins a long and continuous journey, developing the skills and abilities needed to navigate and succeed in using language effectively to make sense of her world. Her success in life literally depends on how well this happens! And it's happening in your home, under your care. Let's spend a brief time thinking about what is happening. Here are six things we need to understand about language, and about reading:

1. This is a long-term developmental process.

As we have noted, children are born with absolutely no language and no set of meanings or concepts about their world. In a few short years, they are speaking with skill and confidence about their world. This happens in your home—but it doesn't happen overnight! As parents, you have the privilege— and the responsibility—and the joy—of walking beside your children as they navigate this long journey.

From the time your child is born, he is bathed in language. You treat your baby as if he is carrying on a conversation with you. You talk to him and coo over him. Other family members or caregivers do the same thing. You talk to the baby all the time. You respond to the noises he makes with detailed and exaggerated responses. The whole setting is about interacting with the baby's sounds. You treat your baby as if he's totally a part of your language world.

Soon random cries, coos, and noises give way to babbling, and major developmental changes begin to take place. The baby utters and practices an impressive assortment of sounds, and you repeat those sounds back to her with words and with exaggerated pronunciations and facial gestures. Think of how we listen for those first sounds of "da" or "mmm" and we start to repeat "Mama" or "Da-Da" or "back to her, along with lots of words and sentences. You listen to see if she tries to imitate you. Some "words" emerge to label things around her, and she can tell how happy that makes the adults around her. She's not saying the word exactly as you say it, but you're so proud of her!

Before long she's using single words to communicate complete ideas, and you can figure out what she means. Two or three-word phrases carry complete language messages. "Mommy go" or "Doggie bye-bye." You interpret her messages and all the time you are helping her learn by restating or expanding what she says and repeating it back to her. It's an intense, on-going language laboratory that is open 24 hours a day, seven days a week, 365 days a year, and both infants and adults love working in the lab!

These activities allow your child to develop a basic vocabulary and the fundamentals of language structure. By age two, your child has hundreds of words in his speaking vocabulary, and even more that he understands. He is constantly talking about all kinds of things!

At the same time children are learning words, they are learning basic language patterns. From the very beginning children are "speaking" in whole thoughts, though early on they may express them with only one or two words. Your child makes sounds, and you respond with whole phrases — "Are you hungry?" "Do you like that?" "Time to change that diaper?" "Where does it hurt?" You are modeling the language that the child will gradually make her own. As time goes on, she uses more complex word patterns as she continues to interact with adults. Over time, she will fill in to create more complete sentence patterns and learn to use the basic conventions of spoken language correctly and powerfully.

It's not important for us to go through all the details of the stages children go through as they develop all the elements of their spoken language. But what is important is that children are growing up in a home where people are engaging them with language and using language to create meaning. This process will continue as they grow and mature. It takes a long time. But the journey takes place in your home. Your child's vocabulary and language development are *directly related* to how often you and others listen to them, talk to them, and do things with them.

What about reading? Just like learning to use language, learning to read is a long-term developmental process, and just like language, learning how to deal with print can also begin very early in a child's life. Even though we sometimes think that learning to read only happens when a child goes to school, the fact is that children can learn a lot about how to handle print from the very beginning of learning language.

When children are exposed to books and printed language early in life, they learn to engage with print as a part of life, not as something that is shoved on them to "make them" learn to read. So the bottom line is simply this: Make print a part of your engagement with your child from the very beginning. Over time, this will have a major impact on how well your child learns to read.

2. The home is the best place for it to happen.

It seems obvious, but learning language only takes place in a social setting, where the child is in continuous and meaningful interaction with other people. What is the fundamental and most important setting for this to take place? The answer is clear. It's your home. The child who is learning to talk at home finds himself in a situation where NOT talking is not an option. Talking is *what's happening*. Everyone around him is talking, a lot of their talk is aimed at him, and they seem to be expecting him to respond. That's the world he lives in. And the people in that world, those who care for him and show him affection, do so in the midst of a constant flow of language. In that environment, learning to talk just happens.

What about reading? Can the home play a vital role in learning to read? The answer is yes! The home can also become a world where social interaction with print happens all the time. Introducing print into a child's life early communicates that dealing with print is a natural part of life. Just like learning to talk, learning to read happens best when it is seen as a normal, expected, fun, and valuable piece of the child's daily fabric of life. The place where this can happen best is in the home, starting from the very beginning.

3. It happens "naturally."

You don't "teach" your child to talk. Children become expert users of the language spoken around them *without formal instruction*. There is no "curriculum" that you follow to make the learning happen. You don't need instructional tools or materials or a textbook, or a particular "method." You don't need to be trained to become a language instructor. You don't need to give tests along the way to see if your child meets performance criteria.

In many ways, you are more an observer and a collaborator than a teacher. Your child is learning language "on your watch," but his actual development comes from a wonderful interaction between his innate mental and social gifts and the environment you provide.

By age four children have acquired most of the elements of adult language. Most parents never think about how this happens, and researchers may not even agree exactly how it works. But very simply, children learn to use language naturally as they grow up in a community of language users.

But what about reading? "Hmmm," you might say. "Learning to read happens naturally? I don't think so. Learning to read was hard work for me in school." Let's explore this idea a little.

Certainly, reading doesn't just "happen" in the same way that language develops. Why not? Well, it's not too hard to see. Oral language is something that is going on all the time all around the developing child. As we have seen, in that kind of environment, children learn to interact with language because that's what their world is all about. Basically, they can't avoid getting involved with using oral language.

With printed language, however, someone has to *show* them how it works. Print is not always a common element in their daily life. When contact with print is involved, someone needs to show them how it works.

This leads to an interesting question: What would happen if print *were* a common part of the developing child's daily life, just like oral language is?

What if children had books and signs and notes all around in their environment? What if adults were always reading to them, and pointing out what print says? What if adults wrote notes for children and read the notes to them, and encouraged them to "write" back? What if adults put up signs and pictures all around the child's environment and read them to the children, and often asked the children to say what they think these things say? What if adults pointed out printed signs on buildings and along the road when their children were in the car or on the bus with them?

Well, I think you get the point. There are many "natural" ways that print can be made a part of a child's world. Will they learn all there is to know about dealing with print in their natural setting? No reading is something that typically needs to be *taught*, and the school will play a central role in helping children learn a variety of skills involved in reading.

However, there is a great deal about reading that children can learn naturally in the home in their everyday interactions with adults. In fact, every year, lots of children enter kindergarten classrooms already knowing how to read, largely because the adults in their environment have made using print a natural part of their daily lives.

Bottom line: Learning to read requires that someone show the child how it's done. That's what happens in school, and it is essential. At the same time, there is much that can happen "naturally" in the home that contributes to a child's learning how to read. We'll be learning more about these things in the rest of the book.

4. The goal is meaning.

As children and adults engage each other through language, what is it they are "languaging" <u>about</u>? It's about life, about what's important to them. Children are not learning language for the sake of learning language. No, they are learning to use language to make sense of the expe-riences they are having, and to meet the needs their lives demand. Their language is the way they can make sense of and communicate the mean-ings of life that is going on all around them. So, when interacting with children, we concentrate on what they are trying to communicate, not on how they communicate.

What about reading? Interestingly, we don't always handle reading this way. When it comes to reading, we sometimes tend to pay more attention to *how the child is doing it* than we do to what the child is getting from reading or the meaning he is creating by reading.

For example, consider two different ways of introducing your child to a book. One way would be to sit down with your child, read the book to her, and along the way point out the characters and actions in the pictures, talk about what is happening in the story, ask questions about what she thinks is going on in the story.

Another way might be to sit down with your child, find the first word, tell him the sound of each letter, ask him to make each sound, then sound out the whole word and pronounce it for you, then proceed to the next word, work your way through all the words in the first sentence the same way, have him "read" the whole sentence, and proceed in this manner through the rest of the book.

Obviously, I have overdrawn and oversimplified the contrast, but the point is important. In the first case, you emphasize the *meaning* of the book— who the characters are, what they look like, what they are saying and doing, and what it all means to your child. In the second case, you emphasize *reading performance*, the act of pronouncing the words.

The two different approaches produce different outcomes. Focusing only on the print and isolated bits and pieces of words will probably not result in meaning. Rather you are expecting your child to *perform*, putting the emphasis on *how* he is reading. Focusing on meaning, however, produces engagement, anticipation, pleasure, and new ideas.

In addition, as your child understands the meaning as you read, he also begins to pay attention to the details of the print and begins to match what he understands with the words he sees. *Meaning* draws the child to the book, and meaning should be the driving force that encourages him to explore print. The bottom line: Learning to read, just like learning to talk, should be about <u>meaning</u>. And that happens best when the child is exploring meaningful print with caring adults in the home.

So, the development of language (and reading) is a long-term developmental process that happens naturally in the home and focuses on making meaning. This leads us to a fifth idea about language and reading development:

5. "Mistakes" are tolerated – even celebrated.

It is often said that one of the most important things about learning anything is that we learn from our mistakes. When it comes to language learning, this is an essential element of the process. One of the joys of interacting with children is to see them trying out words and phrases as they seek to use language. For example, we don't get upset when our toddler says, "See my foots." When my three-year-old granddaughter asked me, "Where you was?" I didn't correct her grammar, I told her where I was! The fact is, it's exciting for us to see children working out the mastery of their language. It's one of the joys of working in the language lab!

What about reading? Do we want to reward the child for making mistakes when reading?" Do we really want your child to read incorrectly? Of course not. But while a child is in the process of learning to read, the question of how you *handle* mistakes needs to be examined.

Let me illustrate with an example. My son was one of those who was reading before he started school. (Just for the record, I made NO attempt to "teach" him to read. It just happened.) Also, to set the record straight, my daughter, born later, did *not* learn to read before entering school, and learning to read didn't come as easily. In any case, here's what happened in our car one day when Steven was three. We were driving near our home in Indiana and came upon a roadside fruit and vegetable stand where a local farmer was selling produce. On the side of the small white wooden build-ing was a sign consisting of a red circle and a green circle, on which were written the words, "Stop and Save." As we approached the stand, from the back seat came a loud yell, "Stop and go!"

How would you react to this? I could have said, "No, Steven, you're *wrong*. It says, 'stop and <u>save</u>.' Can't you see that the word in the green circle starts with an 's' just like the first word does? You need to pay better attention." Well, I'm sure you can guess that's NOT what I said. Rather, my response was, "Good for you!" Why? Because I realized that, far from being "wrong," he was making a very appropriate response based on his developmental stage and his emerging grasp of how print works.

His background included the concept of red and green being related to stopping and going (standard drill for adults with kids in the car when you come to a stoplight), he knew the word "stop" from seeing and iden-tifying it on red stop signs while riding in the car and from books read to him. He had heard the phrase "stop and go" enough to know that the two often go together in English. In short, he had a pretty powerful set of cues to prompt him to think the sign said, "Stop and go."

Did he read the sign "wrong?" In one sense, I suppose you could say so. However, rather than making a "mistake," I would prefer to say that he made a "miscue" and a powerful one at that. I knew two important things about his miscue. First, I knew that this miscue was developmentally appropriate and that it would not persist. I was not worried that he had somehow learned something wrong and was doomed to be a poor reader.

Second, I knew that his miscue told me something about what he knew, how he thought, and how active his mind was in putting concepts together.

Just like oral language, reading "mistakes" occur for a *reason*. We can use them to help us discover what kinds of strategies children are using and find ways to help them become better readers. We'll take a detailed look into what is happening when children are reading in the next section of the book.

In the meantime, consider what would it be like if, just as with spoken language, adults honored children's attempts to make printed language work for them? What would it be like if, instead of seeing "errors" in reading as something to be feared and avoided, children see their attempts to recognize words as challenges they can take on without fear and with a sense of adventure that is recognized and supported by adults? I think you can see what a difference that could make for our children.

Here's one final point about how language develops in the home—and this is huge.

6. There is never an expectation that children are not succeeding.

Think about that for a moment. From the very beginning in the crib, we engage in constant language interactions with our children as if they totally understand us and are responding appropriately to all the language we throw their way. And we act like we totally understand every utterance that comes out of them. We never communicate that we are worried they're not getting it, or that we think they're doing it wrong.

This communicates something very special and important to our children. It tells them that doing language is what's *expected*. It tells them that they *belong* to our language world. It tells them that communicating with language about their experiences—no matter *how* it is done— is the right thing and it's a good thing. It's what they *should* be doing, and we want them to keep it up!

What about reading? This is the one principle about language learning that, unfortunately, many people may have trouble following when it comes to reading. Although parents don't worry that their child won't learn to talk, they sometimes do worry that their children will not learn to read. Children themselves may have a very real fear that learning to read will be hard, and they may not make it. I would like to suggest, however, that the same things that are true of oral language development are also true of reading development.

What if we as adults treated development of using printed language like we do the development of oral language? What if we assumed that children could develop skill in using printed language in the home, just like they do oral language? What if we considered the development of using print to be a "natural" thing for children, just like oral language? What if we had children engage with print without expecting perfection and letting them know that "mistakes" are OK – even good? And, what if we treated children in the home as if we *expected* them to do reading? Building such a culture of literacy in the home is the greatest legacy we can give our children.

So where are we? Where does reading come from? We've learned that reading grows out of strong background of powerful language development. That development takes a long time. It happens naturally in a setting where adults provide a rich background of life experiences and continually engage in meaningful language and exposure to print around those experiences. It happens when adults allow and encourage children to try out all kinds of language and print experiments, and always let children know that their efforts to engage with printed language are valued and expected. That's where powerful reading comes from.

As this process plays itself out in your children, here are two important things to keep in mind: The first is, be patient, and the second is keep pushing. Sounds like a contradiction, doesn't it? But when you think about it, it makes sense.

In the first case, we are patient because we know not to expect perfection as children are learning language. It takes time for children to try out and practice using language. They will get it. But it's a long-term process. And each child is different. So be patient.

At the same time, we want them to always be moving forward. We want to challenge them, to encourage them, to push them to use language as powerfully as they can. So, we keep interacting with our children using all kinds of new words and all kinds of phrases. We keep on expecting them to engage with language in increasingly complex ways about new experiences that we provide them. We're listening to them and talking to them all the time about all kinds of things. That's what they need from us. That's what gives them the incredible *power* of language that they need to succeed – in reading, and in everything else.

So What?

Is your home a place where children are continually engaged in "languaging" about things that are important and meaningful to them? Is it a place where there is lots of talk about important ideas? Where "mistakes" are tolerated? Where there is always the expectation that children will communicate successfully? Where adults celebrate their children's growing language power without undue pressure?

Think about it: What are some things about your home that are really good in terms of promoting language development and lots of learning about the world your children live in?

What are some things you would like to do better in helping your children to develop strong language skills and engagement with their world?

What's Next?

In the next two chapters, I'll go into a little more detail about how language and experience develop in the home and how these two things form the foundation on which reading depends. We'll start by looking at language in Chapter Five.

CHAPTER FIVE:
WHERE DOES WORD POWER COME FROM?

"Words bounce. Words, if you let them, will do what they want to do and what they have to do."

–Anne Carson, *Autobiography of Red*

We have seen that language and experience provide the foundation for successful reading. In this chapter, I want to look deeper into the language element.

As we have pointed out, children *know* language. In fact, children have remarkable language accomplishments early in life. Most children have an active vocabulary of thousands of words by the age of six. Their "active" vocabulary means words they know and use. Children learn thousands of new words every year during their school-age years. By the time a child starts to have a reading teacher in school, he most likely will have heard and said millions of expressions, in a huge variety of language patterns— phrases, sentences, questions, orders, exclamations, songs and the like!

Why is this important to understand? It will help you appreciate what children already bring to reading. You can help them harness the language power they bring to school and avoid the pain that sometimes goes along with learning to read.

Two elements are involved in language: vocabulary and structure.

Vocabulary

A child's vocabulary comes directly from the language she is immersed in daily. I know that sounds obvious, and it is. But it's critical to understand how important it is that your children hear lots and lots of words and that you expect them to use lots of words as well. Words are the way we label and organize the experiences we have, and that's what children do from the beginning of life. And, of course, words are the way they *communicate* about those experiences.

Before words, babies communicate by crying, and soon they squeal and laugh, and if you speak to them all the time, one day they'll reward you by saying a word back! One of the very most important things we can do for our children is to speak to them and with them about all kinds of things, using all kinds of words, all the time. Words are the currency of life, and one of your most important jobs as a parent is to help your child hear and use thousands of words.

Of course, there is a lot of variation in people's vocabularies. Most of us have a large vocabulary of words that we typically use when we are talking. There are also words that we recognize when we hear them, but that we don't typically use when we are talking. And there are words that we can understand the meaning of when we read them, but we've never heard them said and we may never use them in when we talk. Obviously when children are young and first learning to talk, they understand many more words than they actually say. Gradually they learn to use more of the words they have heard and understood.

People's vocabularies also differ because we come from different regions or countries. We have different parents, experiences, education, places of work, and all kinds of other things that influence the words in our vocabulary. Children learn the vocabularies of the people they grow up with. In terms of *how many words*, *which words*, and *what meanings are associated* with those words, there can be huge differences among children when they first start school.

But the bottom-line truth is that the home is the source of vocabulary power. By the time a child enters kindergarten, he will have heard thousands and thousands of words in daily life activities. Reading a book to a child every few days will add thousands more. The impact of hearing and using lots of words in the home is of inestimable value for learning to read.

Structure

Now let's turn to an equally important, but in many ways more fascinating aspect of language—its structure. That is, how words are put together in groups to make communication possible. Different languages are structured in different ways; I'll concentrate on English.

Word order is important in English. If I say, "Going I town to tomorrow am." you might recognize all the words, but you probably stopped for a moment when you read the sentence. And, no doubt, you found yourself rearranging the words in your mind in order to get meaning from the sentence. In English, word order is important.

Here is a key point about word order: *Language is highly predictable.* This matter of predictability will come up often in our discussion of reading. For now, let's just make the basic point. If I say, "I love . . ." what can you predict about the next word? You can't predict the exact word, but you can predict that it is a noun or a noun phrase, because that's what comes in that slot in an English sentence. The English language uses patterns to arrange words in sequences that others can understand. As speakers, children learn early on to use the basic structures of English.

A good illustration of this aspect of the English language is Lewis Carrol's famous poem "The Jabberwocky" from Alice in Wonderland. Here's the well-known first stanza:

'Twas brillig, and the slithy toves

Did gyre and gimble in the wabe;

All mimsy were the borogoves,

And the mome raths outgrabe.

Even though most of the "words" are not <u>real</u> words, you can read this. Why? Because it "works" as English language. You can predict that "brillig" is an adjective describing the conditions, perhaps the weather. You know that "toves" is a plural noun and whatever toves might be, they can be described with the adjective "slithy." And, you also know that toves can "gyre" and "gimble." (Sounds like a new dance!) In this case, even with no experience that brings meaning to these words, you still can read the passage. This is because language structure is patterned, regular and therefore highly predictable.

These patterns are simply commonly agreed on ways of doing language. We can combine and modify the patterns in endless varieties, but we have to stick to the basic commonly accepted patterns, or we don't communicate. Where did these patterns come from? Although that can be a fascinating and complex study, it's not important here. Our language simply is what it is. The good part is that we don't have to study any of this in order to use it. We know it *intuitively*. We know how to speak in English sentences. We've been doing it since we were two years old.

So, what does this have to do with reading? Simply this: Children who have command of a wide variety of sentence structure patterns, who use and understand these patterns and can combine these patterns into lots of language structures, will have a <u>significant</u> advantage when it comes to understanding print — because printed materials use these same patterns.

These are the patterns authors use when they write. And, because these patterns are highly predictable, the reader who is familiar with all kinds of language structures has great **power** to predict and confirm the messages as he reads.

The bottom line is very simple and very important—the child who comes to print with a rich and complex language background, including lots of words in his vocabulary and lots of experience and fluency in constructing and receiving verbal messages, *already possesses* some vital basic tools needed to become an effective reader! On the other hand, the child with limited vocabulary and limited experience using conventional English language patterns is more likely to have difficulties dealing with print.

So What?

So, with all these ideas in mind, think about your home. Here are some ideas to think about as <u>you</u> "language" with your children at home as a part of their natural life:

- Talk to your children—<u>all the time</u>—about <u>everything.</u> For example, when doing something as common and simple as giving your infant or toddler a bath, <u>talk</u> to her, <u>talk</u> about how nice and warm the water is, how the soap smells, how the warm towel feels, etc. Bathing your child is an *experience*. Make the most of the experience by wrapping it in language!

- Make times each day to <u>talk with</u> your children. In other words, <u>plan</u> to have conversations, and when you do, use grown-up words and encourage them to ask you about any words you use that they don't recognize.

- Encourage children to try out and say things without penalty or disrespect. Accept their attempts.

- Use lots of sentence variety in conversations. Explain things in a variety of ways.

- Now and then, put up a famous phrase or saying or quotation for them to think about. Talk with them about what the phrase or saying means. Then, use the phrase in conversations around the house. Help make it a part of their language storehouse.

- Challenge children to say more complex things, not simply short answers—asking them for more detail.

- Play word games of all kinds in normal conversations (finding rhyming words, predicting words, coming up with different words that have the same meaning, etc.).

- Be prepared with a question each day to ask them (questions about themselves and about what's going on in their world, etc.) Listen—and respond.

- Put up a "Word for the Day" on a sign or bulletin board. Encourage children to ask you about it if they don't know it. Have them use it in sentences as often as they can during the day. Maybe have a contest to see who can use the word correctly the most times during the day.

You can think of lots of other ways to engage your child in using language. Once again, you need to be intentional. Think about what is going on around your home and in all aspects of your family life. There are all kinds of ways to naturally enrich your child's language in the context of life in your home. Take advantage of those opportunities and help your child to build a strong and rich command of language.

What's Next?

Chapter Six concentrates on the second critical foundation for reading that is best developed in the home—meaning.

CHAPTER SIX:
WHERE DOES MEANING COME FROM?

"No matter what anybody tells you, words and ideas can change the world."
—Tom Schulman, *Dead Poets Society*

We have examined the idea of language as a foundation for learning to read. Now let's take a look at the other essential foundation – developing meaning. Two points summarize the idea:

(1) When we read, the meaning in the book comes from the reader.

(2) The meaning in the reader comes from experience.

I'll start with some basic ideas about how people learn. We make meaning when we learn. That's what learning is, and all people are learners. We constantly look for and give meanings to the things we come across in our everyday world. Here's how.

When you run into something (that could be an object or a sound or a person or an event), it doesn't magically have some unknown meaning that you have to figure out. You give it meaning. You naturally try to make sense of it. You fit it in with what you already know. You are the one who makes it "mean something."

The way you do this is by mentally comparing it to other experiences you have had before. You notice how it is the same as or different from previous experiences, and your mind attaches some understanding or meaning to it. Depending on the connection between the new thing and your past experience, you may understand it completely or only a little bit. But you automatically come up with some sort of meaning.

For example, if you visit the zoo, you see animals that you've never seen before. Maybe all you know is that they are some kind of animal, or perhaps some kind of bird or bug. But if you have a pet, you can attach much more meaning to that animal. It's a four-year old female brown and white beagle named Maxine with black eyes and one white paw, who likes to play and is always snitching treats. And "Maxine" means more to you than just an "animal" or even "dog" or even "pet." You have all kinds of meaning and memories and feelings wrapped up in her because you have had lots of experiences with her.

You do this best when you have experiences related to things you are interested in, things that are connected with what you already know, or you've done before. When something doesn't fit very easily, you come up with a new way to understand it, making it fit in with what you already know as much as possible.

What's important is that this all happens automatically and without thinking about it. You don't have to stop and decide how to do it.

Just watch a toddler and you will realize that humans have a drive to make sense of our environment. Toddlers are into everything! They touch things, turn them over, study them, smell them, put them in their mouths.

They also watch what you do and boldly put themselves in the middle of the action! "I do it!" is their favorite saying. They want to make every experience their own. Although it is sometimes frustrating to deal with your own toddlers and nearly always tiring, you need to support them as they get around, even babies when they crawl. What I mean is they need freedom to explore. Not unlimited, of course! But let them do it. And talk with them about what they are doing. Tell them the names of things. Tell them the words for the colors they see, the sounds they hear or make, and the objects they pick up or stumble over.

If you need to stop them or correct them to keep them safe or out of trouble, don't just say "No!" or "Stop" or "Don't." Follow up with an explanation. "No. You may not step on the dog. You will hurt him." "Stop. If you touch the stove, it will burn your fingers and they will hurt." "Don't touch Mama's vase. If it falls down it will break, and I will be disappointed." It doesn't matter whether your child understands everything you are saying. He is hearing the words and your tone of voice and seeing your face and connecting them with his experience. He is learning.

Children are born with a natural and powerful drive to learn. This searching for meaning and making meaning for themselves goes on in many ways throughout childhood and, if you help when they are young, throughout their adulthood as well.

As children grow and are exposed to an increasingly wide variety of experiences, these experiences are built together into an amazing and incredibly complex network of ideas and understandings that become "wired" into their minds. And each of us has different "ideas" wired into our minds, even about common experiences.

For example, most Americans probably have an *idea* about "the 4th of July." When I say "the 4th of July," what comes to mind for you? Maybe your idea includes fireworks, picnics, swimming, family get-togethers and lots of fun. Or maybe it includes disappointment because you or your parents had to work on that holiday, and you missed out on things like that. Your idea about that holiday is composed of thousands of sights, sounds, feelings, and experiences that you have had about "4th of July."

Everyone's July 4th idea is *different and unique* because our *experiences* are different. We have experienced this event in different places, with different people, and under different circumstances. Some of our experiences were wonderful. Some were not. Some of our experiences were joyful and happy, while others may have been frightening, or hard or even tragic.

At the same time, we share enough common experiences about the 4th of July that we can share an understanding what that term "means." We also experience it through schoolbooks and maybe movies or TV shows or video games sporting events. There is some sort of collective idea about it.

Our own "ideas" about things constantly *grow and change*. Your child's idea for July 4th at age two might be a vague sense of loud noises and bright lights in the sky or sparklers in the yard or street. As your child has a July 4th holiday every year, her idea grows and maybe changes. There may be new places and new events that shape her idea—sights, sounds, experiences, exciting or disappointing. New experiences are added, and old ideas are changed. Some experiences become less important while others become more memorable. This process goes on throughout life.

These "ideas" we have are *connected to* our other ideas. Ideas connect and interact and build new ideas. Your child's idea about "4th of July" connects with her idea about "summer" and "America" and maybe "family" and "fun" or "vacation" or "sad" or thousands of other ideas. It's impossible to fully appreciate what our brains are capable of. But we do know that the more variety of experiences your child will have, the greater the number of ideas her mind will create.

What does all this have to do with reading? When your child comes across a printed word, how will she gain meaning? For any printed word— the word "baseball"— or the word "broccoli"—or the word "sports"— or the word "penguin" or "swim" or "block" or ANY word—how does your child gain <u>meaning</u>? Remember, he is bringing the meaning to the word! So, he gains meaning through the *ideas* he has built around that world through his *experiences* in life. The word triggers an automatic, immediate rush of interconnected ideas in his brain.

BUT … this will ONLY happen if he has <u>had</u> those experiences! And where is most important place for those experiences to happen and become part of your child's storehouse of meanings and ideas? I hope I don't have to tell you!

To pull things together—where does meaning comes from?

- When we read, meaning actually comes from the <u>reader</u>, not from the book.

- The meaning that exists in the reader comes from the <u>experiences</u> the reader has had.

- Different readers may have different meanings for words because their experiences are different.

- Meanings grow and change as we continue to have more and more experiences.

- Readers who get the most from reading are the ones who continually enrich their meanings by having new experiences and talking about them with others.

So What?

Based on understanding where meaning comes from, what are some things you can keep in mind as you interact with your children?

- Obviously, <u>provide your children with lots of experiences</u>. This doesn't mean you have to provide elaborate experiences, but it does mean you have to be *thoughtful* and *intentional.* A trip to the hardware store to pick up some wood screws is an experience. Think about ways you could challenge your child to make the experience engaging and <u>talk</u> with her about it as you go.

- Some experiences require travel or other special assistance to make them happen. As a parent or relative or friend, you can help children experience things that they couldn't experience on their own. Find out what's going on in your community and plan to be a part of some of those activities with your children. For example, fairs, parades, volunteering, celebrations, library events, holiday events, out-of-school activities sponsored by schools, etc.

- Children and adults should experience things *together*, and adults should *talk* and *interact* with children about these experiences. Ask your children to describe an experience, and you describe it as well. Ask them how this experience compares to another one. There are hundreds of ways in which conversation about an experience can take place. The more you talk about it, the more meaning the children can draw from when they read. When you have new experiences with your child, plan in advance to have some <u>words</u> related to the experience that you can use as you enjoy it together.

- Have your child caption pictures you took of an experience and write a brief note to family members far away talking about the experience.

- Take time to <u>recall</u> experiences you have had together and <u>compare</u> them with new experiences you have together.

- These days, we're not confined only to experiences we can have directly. The digital world allows us to experience things from all times and places. Engage your child in meaningful explorations of ideas and experiences via the internet. Your local library probably has a large volume of movies, TV, eBooks and audiobooks for all ages that you can stream or download and play later even if you don't have Wi-Fi at home. You can find children's shows for your youngest children, movies or TV shows from many sources including places you would otherwise have to pay for. There are materials on all kinds of topics—nature, art, music, places, historical events. You can experience all kinds of things with your children that you may not get to do in person. And always remember to *share* and *talk about* those experiences with the child.

As you think about life in <u>your</u> home, what are some other ways you can think of that provide rich experiences for your children?

What's Next?

I hope you can appreciate the importance of language and experience as we have examined what reading is all about in the last three chapters. To end this section of the book, we are going to take an interesting look at the encounter between the author and the reader to see how all these ideas play a part in successful reading.

CHAPTER SEVEN:
THE GRAND MEETING

"Readers are often fans of authors, but I, myself, am a fan of readers. They are the ones who breathe life into the pages that we give birth to, after all."

–Janae Mitchell

In the past two chapters, we have seen that successful reading depends on two things: (1) the reader has to have a good command of *language*, and (2) the reader has to have strong background of *experiences*.

I want to take a few minutes to look at the big picture. We are going to jump into the middle of the continuous and lively interaction that is the heart of successful reading – the place where author and reader meet on the printed page. We'll see how these elements – language and experiences — affect how reading happens. Take a look at the illustration on page 47. What's happening?

Here we see the author (writer) and the reader. They don't know each other and probably have never met. Both of them live in their own unique world of **experiences**. From those experiences, each of them has constructed a huge set of **meanings**. Those meanings are stored in their brains in a vast collection of concepts that interact with each other to produce all kinds of thoughts, ideas, understandings and feelings.

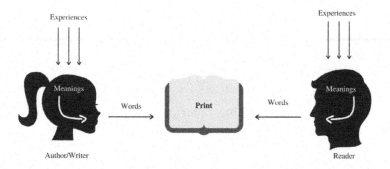

The author and the reader are able to *express* those meanings by using **words**. If the author and the reader were to sit down and talk, they could, by talking and listening to each other, share meanings, explore ideas, and generate all kinds of new meanings together. That's what people do when they interact with each other verbally.

But in the case of reading, the author and the reader don't actually meet face to face and talk. Instead, each of them uses **print** — a way of putting speech into visual symbols. The author chooses words that express the meanings she wants to express and puts those words down in print. The reader recognizes those printed words and gives them meanings that he has come to associate with them.

Don't miss the amazing power of this transaction. Using nothing but a series of marks on a piece of paper, the reader and the writer are able to share and to shape all kinds of ideas, understandings, and emotions. When we think about this, we begin to understand the incredible value of print in our world, and the absolute necessity of learning to use print wisely and well.

We have seen that many things can affect how this transaction goes. For example, what if the background experiences of the author are different than the background experiences that the reader brings to print? The author uses words that depict her background experiences, but the reader's background experiences may lead him to give the same words somewhat different meanings.

Is this a problem? It can possibly present some minor challenges. But it's also possible that such differences may cause the reader to gain new insights because he is forced to think about meanings in a new way – a way that may never have come in any other setting.

The same is true when authors and readers have different language backgrounds. The author may use words and phrases to express meaning in a way that is somewhat unusual to the reader who may come from a different language background. Is this a problem? Again, it can present a minor challenge. On the other hand, it is often the case that an author expresses an idea in language that challenges the reader to think, and thus to create or unlock a whole new meaning or insight that now becomes a part of the reader's world.

What is happening during reading is a fascinating mixing of experiences, ideas, and understandings. Authors work hard to use language that communicates their experience and meaning background. And readers, by being exposed to the author's words, can be moved to discover new understandings that expand their worlds in significant ways. In short, reading allows us to grasp a world of meanings that we can never attain through direct experience alone, but is opened to us through print.

Why have I asked you to spend these few minutes thinking about how authors and readers meet in print? I believe it helps us to see how important it is that we provide rich experiences and strong language backgrounds for our children in our homes. Thinking about what is happening during reading can give us some important insights into what is happening when our children are engaged in reading.

So What?

Spend a little time thinking about the picture of the writer and reader. What are some important ideas and experiences that you may never have been able to gain if it hadn't been for reading? As you consider this, what are some things you want to be sure to do for your children to help them take the most advantage of interacting with writers?

What's Next?

We have just seen that everything that is going on in reading winds up in *print*. Print is where the writer and the reader meet. Obviously, it's essential that the reader is able to know what words the print stands for. How do readers figure out what the print is saying? How do readers recognize those printed words? That's where we are going in Part Three of the book.

PART THREE:
GOING DEEPER

I hope you have a better understanding of what reading is all about, and I hope that you have been challenged to think about the ways you can help your child develop the two fundamental tools that lead to proficient reading: language and experience. At the same time, I'm guessing you might still be wondering about what exactly is going on when your child is working his way through print. In this section of the book, we will take a closer look into the reading process itself and describe some interesting and important ideas about what is happening when your child is confronting those words on the printed page. Let's take a closer look.

CHAPTER EIGHT:
UNLOCKING PRINT

"Reading is to the mind what exercise is to the body."
–Joseph Addison

Before we get started, take a minute and go back to the picture of the author and the reader in our last chapter. Look at all the arrows. Where do they all wind up pointing to? We see that everything winds up pointing to **print.** No matter how much experience or language the reader brings to the encounter, no matter what ideas the author possesses, all of it winds up being captured in a set of marks placed on a page or other surface. Somehow those visual marks need to be translated into *words* and sentences for successful reading to happen.

We've all heard the expression "where the rubber meets the road." It refers to that time or place in any activity when something has to happen to make the whole thing work. In reading, this is the time when the reader encounters printed words and has to somehow figure out what those words are. In many ways—and particularly for the child who is first learning to read— that often seems to be all we think reading is about.

Unlike the development of oral language, recognizing words in print is not something that just happens naturally in the course of growing up. It's something that needs to be *learned*. So how do children learn to recognize words in print? The answer to that question is not simple, but it is understandable. That's what this chapter is about.

We will examine seven basic questions:

1. What's the ultimate goal?

2. What's the foundation for learning how to deal with print?

3. What's the challenge the reader faces?

4. What's the advantage the reader brings to the task?

5. What's the catch we need to keep in mind?

6. What's the journey of learning to recognize words like?

7. What's the prize that comes when you learn to do this well?

The Goal

The ultimate goal is simple — that the reader *recognizes printed words instantly by sight.* That's the way you and I as mature readers do it. We see words on the page, and we know them without having to stop and figure them out. With very few exceptions, this happens automatically. Mature readers have gotten that way through lots of "doing reading." By repeatedly performing reading tasks in the course of everyday living, we have become so familiar with the words we see over and over again that we recognize them instantly by sight. That's the goal.

The Foundation

Reaching this goal begins with the very important introduction to *basic concepts about print.* Adults lay this critical foundation for children by reading *to them* and reading *for them* from the very early stages of their lives. This happens naturally when we call attention to the print all around us and read it out loud to children. When you read lots of books to young children, you talk with them, ask questions, point out pictures, repeat phrases, and interact about the book. As this is happening, children realize that those marks on the page are the *words* you are saying as you are reading. They come to understand that the words are made up of sets of *letters* that are arranged from *left to right*. These concepts set the stage for learning to identify words as they are being read. Very often, children who are read to a lot begin to recognize words on their own long before any formal teaching of reading occurs.

The Challenge

As children are introduced to the concept of print, the issue becomes "how do they figure out what those words are?" How do they identify and recognize printed words when they see them on the page? That's the challenge.

Meeting this challenge involves focusing attention on the printed words using all the tools in the reader's possession, including analytic or "decoding" tools, and clues that come from the fund of knowledge and language that the reader brings to the task.

In the early stages of learning to read, the heart of the challenge is learning skills to *decode* individual printed words. That means recognizing the letters that make up the printed word and associating them with sounds that can be put together to predict what the word is—what we know as *phonics*. There is lots of variety in how different sounds are spelled in the English language, so phonics doesn't always work perfectly for every possible situation. But learning basic phonic skills is an important starting point for meeting the challenge of identifying words in print.

Decoding words phonetically doesn't just come naturally. It requires instruction So this aspect of the challenge needs to be addressed by clear teaching in the early grades through a well-structured school program or in-home curriculum. It is not a goal of this book to attempt to describe all the details about how phonics should be taught or to provide or suggest a particular phonics program. However, as a parent, it is good to learn as much as possible about the phonics program that is being used with your child so you can wisely support your child's efforts.

If reading were only a matter of figuring out individual words in isolation, phonics would seem to be the only solution. But reading means recognizing words as they appear in phrases and sentences and paragraphs. This means that readers bring other strategies to bear as they attempt to recognize printed words.

For one thing, the *flow of language* in which a word is found often suggests what the word might be. We have noted earlier that the English language is very *predictable*. That is, we expect certain kinds of words to occur in predictable ways in sentences. Noticing what kind of word might be expected in a sentence doesn't tell you exactly what the word is, but it gives you some good possibilities that help you predict what that word might be.

Still another cue might come from the *context* or the meaning surrounding the sentence. When readers are paying attention to the *meaning* of what they are reading, that can often have a powerful effect on helping them figure out what an unrecognized word most likely is. Certain words "make sense" in the context and thus are more likely to be correct than other words. Obviously, this cue, like the other cues, isn't perfect. But it helps the reader narrow down the possibilities, and when put together with other cues can help lead to successful recognition of the word.

So, there are at least three kinds of cues that might help meet the challenge by suggesting what an unrecognized word is – cues that come from the *sounds* of the letters in the word, cues that come from the *flow of the language*, and cues that come from the *context or meaning* of what you are reading.

These strategies are not perfect. They don't *guarantee* that a word will be correctly identified every time, but what is amazing, and wonderful, is that our brains are able to process these cues and to *combine* them. The brain allows these different cues *to work together*, and to do so *quickly*, and without specifically thinking about it.

Here's the challenge. When a reader comes to a word he doesn't immediately recognize, can he identify cues that come from the letter sounds, the flow of language, and the meaning context, and then use those cues to come up with a good prediction of what that word probably is? It's a challenge all children need to face when learning to read.

Though a significant part of the response to meeting this challenge—phonic decoding—requires formal instruction, it's important to note that much of the power for figuring out what words are comes from the home environment. An environment that is language rich—an environment in which those around the child are using language all the time, using all kinds of language patterns, and expecting the child to be engaged with language at a high level—is clearly where the home becomes an important source of reading power for the child.

Likewise, the power to use meaning or context cues comes from living in an environment in which the child is exposed to and involved in lots of experiences, and these experiences are shared and discussed freely. In other words, much of the "context" comes from the child's home life. A child whose life is rich in meaning because all kinds of experiences are engaged in at home adds to the likelihood of recognizing printed words successfully.

The Advantage

There's an advantage that readers bring with them when confronting words they don't immediately recognize. That is, in the vast majority of cases, they *already know how to pronounce the word*. As we have noted before, most of the words readers encounter in print are words that are already in their listening/speaking vocabulary. This means that the child is typically not on a quest to discover some deep unknown secret, but rather to recognize the word as something he already knows and uses naturally. The brain is able to put cues together in powerful ways, especially when the word is one that is already familiar to the reader in speech and hearing. Once again, we see how important the home is in providing a strong language base for children.

The Catch

You will notice that I've used the work "prediction" when using these cues. There's a reason for that. The fact is that none of these cueing systems *guarantee* that the reader will *absolutely* come up with the *correct* word *every single time*. That's the catch. While learning how to recognize unknown words, children will make mistakes. That's not bad. It's just the way things are. We all do it.

So, don't expect perfection. Just like learning anything else, mistakes are a part of the learning process. In fact, it's often the mistakes that help us figure out a better response. We learn from our mistakes, and this is certainly true of learning to read. One of the things to look for when children are reading is whether or not they self-correct when they choose a word that doesn't work, showing that they are paying attention to meaning while using the cues available to them to make right choices.

The Journey

We need to see this matter of identifying printed words realistically. It takes <u>time</u> to become good at recognizing words quickly and efficiently. And it takes lots of <u>practice</u>. Think of it as a *journey* that your child is taking. At the beginning of the journey, he may have very few words that he recognizes instantly as whole words, so most words he has to work at to identify, as we have described above. That's the challenge. But what happens as a child continues to work through the challenge of identifying printed words? Things change! That's the journey. Let's look at a couple of things that happen along the way.

First, the child gets better at using those cues and figuring out words. Very simply, the more she does it, the better she gets at it. She becomes more efficient and more accurate in deciding what words match the sounds and language flow and the meaning of what she is reading, so she gets better and better at recognizing words more and more quickly.

Another important thing happens along the journey. As children are working their way through print using these tools to help them identify words, more and more words become "sight vocabulary" for them, especially words that occur with a high frequency in printed materials. The more they read, the more they encounter certain words over and over again. Gradually they find that they recognize those words without having to stop and "figure them out." This, as we have said, is the ultimate goal. Put simply, the more they read, the more they encounter words, and the more they encounter words, the more these words become instantly recognizable as sight vocabulary.

And this allows the child to make use of another common way to recognize unfamiliar words – by comparison, or analogy. There are many words that look alike in print. As some of these words becomes a part of the child's sight vocabulary, it becomes very easy to quickly recognize other words in the family because they look alike. For example, if a child knows the word "look" in print, words like "cook," "hook," and "brook" are often easy to figure out quickly. Again, this happens naturally as more and more words are encountered.

It's important to understand that children do not all follow the same exact path in making this journey, and not all children make the journey at the same pace. There are some children who will grasp the skills of recognizing words very quickly with very little help needed. Other children need lots more time and lots more practice to master these skills.

We need to be sensitive to the differences among children and help them follow this path at their own pace and exercising their own capacities. But whatever the unique path or pace is involved, children need to know that it is a journey they *will* complete, and one that we will be walking alongside them.

To sum up the journey: The process of learning how to identify unknown words takes time and practice. The journey begins when children are read to, and they recognize that the marks on the page represent the words that are being read to them. As children go through the process of learning and using cues to identify words, more and more words become "sight" vocabulary for them, which is the ultimate goal. Children vary in terms of how they master the process and how fast they go through the journey, but they will make it. The journey is a temporary fact of learning to read. They will get through it and will come to a point when they are able to identify thousands and thousands of words as wholes with speed and power.

The Prize

So where does all this lead? Certainly, it allows the child to meet the goal we have outlined—being able to recognize words instantly by sight. But the real prize lies beyond this achievement. The real prize is that by making this journey, the child becomes free to focus completely on meaning, and thus to experience all that reading can do for him. Without the hassle of having to repeatedly stop and figure out what an unrecognized word is, the reader is free to concentrate on what he is reading, why he is reading, and what reading can do for him.

This makes the whole power of reading available. Reading enables us to perform the daily tasks of life effectively. Reading introduces us to new experiences and new ideas. Reading brings us new levels of joy and insight into the world we live in. In short, reading is a crucial bridge to participating in life effectively. That's the prize children receive as they become effective readers.

Let's quickly review what this issue of children learning to recognize words in print is all about:

- The <u>goal</u> is for the child to be able to pronounce words immediately by sight.

- The <u>foundation</u> is laid when a child exposed to print and comes to recognize that what he sees on the page stands for the words he is hearing.

- The <u>challenge</u> is for the child to be able to use a variety of cues as quickly and effectively as possible to figure out what an unrecognized word is when he comes to it.

- The <u>advantage</u> is that in most cases, the child *already knows* how the word is pronounced.

- The <u>catch</u> is that the child will sometimes make mistakes.

- The <u>journey</u> is a necessary path that takes time and practice to follow.

- The <u>prize</u> is that the child becomes free to use reading to affect her whole life in powerful ways.

So What?

From the point of view of a young child in the process of learning to read, this matter of figuring out printed words on the page is typically seen as the major issue. It is the single and most obvious task that the child must conquer. I hope that our discussion of what's involved in learning to recognize printed words has been helpful in understanding what this challenge is all about and has helped you appreciate what your child might be going through in the process of learning to read.

But more than that, I hope this has given you a perspective that allows you to come alongside your child, realizing that there are ways to navigate print successfully, and to know that your child will make it and can experience a world of meaning through the power of print.

What's next?

In our next chapter, we are going to take a closer look at what is happening when children are in the process of working to identify printed words that they don't immediately recognize. We'll take a peek into the process and see what can happen, and what it means. By the end of this next chapter, you should have a very complete understanding of what can happen and what questions you might still have.

CHAPTER NINE:
A CLOSER LOOK—WATCHING IT HAPPEN

"There are many little ways to enlarge your world. Love of books is the best of all."

– Jacqueline Kennedy

In our last chapter, our goal was to understand more about what is very often the most challenging and stressful aspect of learning to read for children—seeing the printed words on the page and figuring out "what they say." We know that our children will reach the ultimate goal of recognizing words by sight. But we also know that there is no "magic bullet" or easy way to make this happen. This is simply a part of reading that everyone masters as a part of learning to read. That's just the way it is.

In this chapter, we'll take a closer look at what that journey is like. This should help us understand better what might be going on when our children are dealing with print, and how we might be helpful to them.

Word Recognition in Action

In describing the "challenge" in the last chapter, we said that there are at least three kinds of cues that might help a reader identify a word she doesn't recognize by sight. Let's try to illustrate what it might be like for that reader. We'll peek in on a child who is in the process of doing reading. We'll call her Alicia. Alicia is not a beginning reader who is just learning to read. She already recognizes lots of words by sight. What we want to see is what might happen when she comes to a word she *doesn't* recognize in print while she is reading.

Here's a part of the passage Alicia is reading:

Caleb was pretty sure that the thief was hiding on the other side of the fence. Caleb peeked over the fence.

Let's assume that Alicia is reading and doesn't immediately recognize the word "peeked." What does she do? What *can* she do? How might Alicia figure out how to "read" that word? Actually, there are several things Alicia might do. Let's take a look at them.

Using Letter-Sound ("phonics") Cues

We might guess that Alicia's first instinct is to "sound out" the word. The beginning letter "p" comes naturally if you just start to say the letter name. The two "e" letters also prompt the natural sound, as does the closing of the throat when you say the name of the letter "k." With these sounds, Alicia has a good chance to come up with the pronunciation of the word, especially if the word "peeked" is a word that is in her listening/speaking vocabulary.

Using Language Cues

If Alicia doesn't immediately recognize the word by sound, what else might happen? For one thing, her sense of language might suggest what the word might be. That is, she might predict that the word is a verb—an action word—because that's the kind of word that comes in this place. The sentence says, "Caleb _____ over the fence." Several words *could possibly* work in that place. (Caleb <u>jumped</u>, Caleb <u>fell</u>, etc.). Alicia's sense of how English sentences naturally flow tells her that there are a limited number of words that "fit" in this place in the sentence. This helps her narrow down her possible choices for predicting what the unknown word is. If Alicia combines her thoughts about possible words that fit with her sense of what sounds the letters make, her chances of identifying the word correctly become even greater.

Using Meaning (Context) Cues

As she is reading, Alicia is also thinking of the context and meaning of what she is reading. In this case, knowing that the thief was hiding on the other side of the fence, she might think Caleb would want to be careful, like maybe trying to get a look at the thief without being seen himself. This processing of the meaning of what she is reading naturally prompts Alicia to consider words that make sense in this situation, and thus adds to the likelihood of determining correctly what the word is.

This illustration is provided to show some of the possible strategies a child might use to figure out a word she doesn't recognize – thinking about what the word might sound like, thinking about what kind of word fits in flow of the sentence, and thinking about what word might make sense in the context. Using some or all of these cues, Alicia most likely can predict that the word is probably "peeked." Good for you, Alicia. Keep on reading!

Does it *always happen* this way? No. Does a child *always* use all of the strategies? No. Can we *always* tell what strategies a child is using to figure out a word? No. Is the child *always aware* of what strategies he is using to figure out a word? No. Is the child *always successful* in coming up with the right word? No. But as we said when we outlined the "challenge," our brains are able to use these different kinds of cues together in the moment to come up with a good idea of what the word is. Understanding what is happening gives us a picture of some of the things a child might be going through and can help us understand how we can be helpful.

When a reader does come up with a different word than the one printed, it can be interesting to look at the "miscue" and see what it tells us. In the Appendix, there are a few examples that illustrate what might be behind a child's misidentification of a word while reading. I encourage you to take some time after completing this chapter to read through these examples.

So What?

In this chapter, we have tried to illustrate what it's like for a reader to encounter an unknown word in print and to see what happens when trying to figure out what that word is. I hope you have noticed that much of the source of power to recognize words comes from what happens in the child's home environment – strong language proficiency and a rich background of meaningful experiences. To summarize, the journey involves:

- Attending to the sounds of letters in words to help predict what unrecognized words might be.
- Attending to the flow of language to help predict what unrecognized words might be.
- Attending to the context and meaning to help predict what unrecognized words might be.
- Using these cues together to come up with the best possible choices and continuing to read.
- Continually recognizing more and more words by sight
- Eventually coming to the point where nearly all words are recognized instantly by sight without having to stop and figure out what a word is.

As we travel along with the child on this journey, here are some things we need to keep in mind:

- Using these strategies together is something that takes place in the reader's mind as she is reading. It may not be obvious how she determines what she thinks a particular word is.

- The process is not perfect. For a variety of reasons, the reader may come up with a word other than the one on the page. Miscues (mistakes) happen. It's part of the process, and readers will often self-correct as they continue reading and recognize the mistake.

- The goal should always be meaning. Figuring out how to pronounce words is the means to an end, not an end in itself.

Knowing what we do about how a child may be dealing with unrecognized words, how can we as parents be helpful? Here are some thoughts:

The first thing to keep in mind is to only help when help is clearly needed and desired. It's not our job to teach children everything they need to know about how to use various clues to recognize words. Our job is simply to help and encourage them when they clearly need it. If the child is highly interested and motivated and engaged, we probably don't have to encourage her. In fact, attempts to "help" will most likely be unwelcome interruptions.

On the other hand, if a child happens to be struggling over words and seems to want help, give it naturally and in a way that supports and encourages her to see if she can figure it out. Ask questions like "What word do you think it is? What word fits here? Does it sound like a word you know? If you were the author, what word would you put there? What word makes sense there? Does it look like a word you know?"

Obviously, you don't ask all these questions! The point is that by talking with the child about how he is figuring things out, you are encouraging him to engage what he knows about sounds and about language flow and what he has picked up from the context to make a good prediction about what the word is. The emphasis is not on what the child did "wrong," but on celebrating the joy of figuring out what the word is. Practice in this process is what is needed to give the child a sense of independence and power in reading.

Such interaction can make it something of a game that becomes a fun challenge. Children need to know they are free to use a variety of strategies to figure out print. The more they do it, the better they become at it, and the more efficient their reading becomes. Be sensitive and give the most appropriate help. The key to deciding what is appropriate is that it should help the child keep *reading for meaning*.

Very often—especially when the child is really *engaged* in reading for personal pleasure or to meet a personal need—it's simply best to just *tell* the child what the word is. There's nothing wrong with that. You don't need to worry that by telling him what the word is you have somehow lost a critical opportunity to "teach" that word. Rest assured, he will encounter that word many, many times more. And who knows? Telling him the word might just be the kick he needs to help him remember that word and recognize it by sight from now on.

The bottom line is that you help a child most when you offer help that (1) promotes the goal of reading for meaning, (2) encourages the child to try his own strategies, and (3) is quick and doesn't distract him or interrupt the flow of reading.

I hope this makes what is happening on the journey more understandable and will give you a better sense of what your child is going through. The better we understand the process, the more helpful we can be for our children.

What's Next?

In our next chapter, we will spend some time looking at another important aspect of using print that is an integral part of the journey toward word recognition, and that is writing. How does writing fit into the child's developing mastery of dealing with printed words?

CHAPTER TEN:
WRITING AND READING

"There is more treasure in books than in all the pirate's loot on Treasure Island."
–Walt Disney

In the previous two chapters, we have looked at the process that children go through in learning to recognize words in print and tried to illustrate a little bit of what is happening as they work to figure out what those words on the page are. We have spent much time emphasizing that reading is a language process and as such it is intimately tied up with the development of oral language. It's time we pay attention to the other critical aspect of language—writing.

In this chapter, we will explore how learning to write is related to learning to read and how we can help our children gain the most from an environment that includes lots of writing.

It's important to talk about writing because writing is an integral part of the whole language development process. Reading and writing are not the same, but they are highly related. Reading and writing have also been described as *reciprocal* processes. In many ways, reading and writing are inseparable.

The strategies children use to read are, in some sense, the same ones they use to write. As children function as writers they also function as readers, as they are continually reading and rereading during writing.

They get practice in recognizing and writing the letters of the alphabet. They get practice in creating letter equivalencies for words, giving them multiple opportunities to see how letter-sound relationships work. They write words multiple times, leading to increased automatic recognition of high-frequency words. They practice constructing meaningful sentence patterns. These and other benefits come from doing lots of writing. We know that better writers tend to be better readers, and better readers produce better writing.

We have noted that the ability to use language, at least in terms of oral language (listening and speaking), develops as a natural part of growing up within our social settings. And, we have noted that reading development can be enhanced in much the same way as oral language development, given a positive interactive environment. As you might expect, writing development can also be encouraged and developed in similar ways. In fact, an environment in which listening, speaking, reading and writing are all seen as valuable and expected behaviors is a singularly critical factor in producing literate children.

However, it is important to note one critical difference between oral and written language development. Whereas oral language development occurs pretty much without our specific attention or intention, this is not the case when dealing with the written form of language. When it comes to graphic representation of language (reading and writing), specific attention and intention is required. Simply put, as language users develop, they need someone to show them "how to do it" with regard to decoding and encoding (reading and writing) graphic or written forms of their oral language.

Just like oral language and reading, learning to write is a long-term developmental process that occurs best within a natural interactive social context. Just like speaking and reading, writing is a "whole-to-part" process in which children, guided by the overall goal of making meaning, continuously refine and perfect their skills over time. And, just like oral language and reading, learning to write is most likely to occur when writing is continuously modeled, when "mistakes" are tolerated, when the emphasis is placed on meaning, and there is a pervasive expectation that the child will be successful.

Although they certainly need instruction, a lot of what helps children become good readers and writers is simply engaging them is doing what readers and writers do, and by behaving as if they are skilled language users. As caring adults, we supply children with the *reason* to read and write, the *opportunity* to read and write, and many of the *tools* needed to read and write by simply providing them with an environment that promotes reading and writing. What does this mean? Let's take a brief look at three ways that caring adults can provide environments that use writing to help children become powerful readers.

A "print-rich" environment

Imagine for a moment that a child spends lots of time in an environment which includes:

- Labels for some common objects in the environment
- A message board with daily simple messages to the child
- A place for the child to write messages back.
- Pictures with places for the child to write a label or caption.
- Age-appropriate word and letter games
- Copies of child-authored notes, cards, letters, etc.
- Charts and lists (colors, numbers, alphabet, favorite foods, etc.)
- Age-appropriate books
- Words to favorite songs
- Materials for writing, making signs or books, creating posters, etc.

- Labeled containers for the child's belongings.

- Digital devices on which the child can construct and decode verbal messages.

The list could go on and on. The point is simply that children generally learn to act in ways that are prompted by and appropriate to the environment in which they spend most of their time. If their environment is exclusively devoted to only audio and video communication, that's what they will come to consider the only norm. What we hope they will see, however, is an environment in which print, in all its various forms, is being employed and enjoyed in personally relevant ways.

A "print-productive" environment

A print-rich environment, however, has to be "real." It has to be there for a *reason*. In other words, labels need to be prepared at opportune times when curiosity about something can be satisfied by giving it a printed "name." Written messages to the child need to be *real* messages about personally meaningful things. Children need to be encouraged to write messages to friends and family; those messages need to be sent or delivered, and responses displayed and read together. Word and letter games need to be played and celebrated. Charts and lists need to be constructed for real purposes, then used, updated, revised, and recreated as tasks are accomplished and new ideas come into focus.

The point should be clear. From the perspective of the child, the whole point of the print-rich environment has nothing to do with learning to read and write. The purpose is to carry on the business of communicating about life, attending to those things that are needful or helpful or interesting in the child's life—and using *print* as a primary means of expressing those important things. The print environment is to be productive—generating real communication about real ideas. In the process, the child— acting like a skilled language user and doing the things that readers and writers do—naturally develops and refines the skills of reading and writing.

A "print-safe" environment

Finally, it is important to be reminded that reading and writing development is a long-term process. In the case of writing, beginning with random scribbles and pictures and progressing to formal letters and words and sentences. It is critical that during this process the child knows that it's OK to communicate with whatever tools she currently has at her command.

Someone has said, "What I say I can write. What I write I can read." A child needs to know that the "letter" she wrote to Grandma, even though there is not one correctly written word on the page, is nevertheless a real letter, that she "wrote" it, and that grandma can "read" it (with her help, of course).

When a child spends much time in an environment in which print is constantly present and being used for real and vital purposes with freedom to pursue meaning without penalty for not being perfect, that child has the *opportunity* and the *reason* to develop meaningful literacy skills. And, in the process, he will develop many of the needed *tools* to be effective as well. Writing is a powerful and critical part of the process of becoming literate. Writing needs to go hand in hand with reading as children grow in their ability to use written language to carry out and enrich their lives.

With all this being said, it must be remembered that writing must be *taught*. Children need to go through the process of learning how to form letters and words. This is clearly one of the important activities that takes place in school. As parents and supportive adults, we can reinforce what is happening in the school by helping children to practice the work they are given in the school's writing program. By writing *for* them and *with* them, we expand their opportunities to grasp the relationship between spoken and written language. More importantly, by providing children a print-rich environment, a print-productive environment, and a print-safe environment, we help ensure that there are reasons and opportunities to use those writing tools they are taught at school to enrich their lives.

Our treatment of writing has been necessarily brief, as our primary focus in this book is on reading. However, it's important to note (and should by now be obvious) that much of what we have discussed in terms of the nature of reading and reading development is also true of writing and writing development. Most importantly, it is crucial to emphasize that reading and writing complement and reinforce each other. In a literate environment, it doesn't make sense to have one without the other, and the natural blending of reading and writing in a child's life leads to a more complete and powerful grasp of literacy and literate behavior.

So What?

Make writing a natural and pervasive part of your home environment. Just like developing reading, this requires that you be *intentional*. Many of the things that support writing in the home don't "just happen" naturally. They take time and attention. Be creative! Here are three basic things to do. In keeping with your child's developmental level:

1. Write **to** your child. Let him know that print is a natural way to communicate.

2. Write **with** your child. Show her how writing works. Help her experience the act of putting ideas into print.

3. Write **for** your child. Even if he's not yet able to do writing on his own, let him see it happen with his own words.

What's Next?

We have dealt with many important ideas in this section. In Chapter Eleven, we are going to step back and pull those ideas together. Then we will try to answer some of the questions that might have come up in your mind as you have been reading..

CHAPTER ELEVEN:
LET'S TALK—PUTTING IT ALL TOGETHER

*"Reading is a discount ticket
to everywhere."*
–Mary Schmich

The previous three chapters have been devoted to understanding what is happening as our children are learning to recognize printed words. Here are some key concepts that emerge from our discussion of learning to read:

1. Reading is *language* processes. That is, reading is all about something that children *already know*. It's not a new, foreign or alien thing they are dealing with. Their language is an intimate and pervasive part of who they are.

2. Because this is so, language in print is *highly predictable*. We need to build on the power that comes from the fact that they already know the language, instead of concentrating *only* on the fact that they don't yet recognize all the words in printed form. This notion that print is predictable is key.

3. Reading is an *active* and *constructive* process. Words and meanings don't reside on the page and somehow jump out and do something to the reader. The reader must take the initiative. The

reader must actively seek to recognize words and actively invest those words with meanings. The reader *constructs* meaning as he reads. Based on the tools that the reader brings to the task, and the reader's purpose for reading, each reader builds a unique meaning as he/she processes print.

4. Reading is an *interactive* process. Reading is not just a simplistic, linear, mechanical process of pronouncing individual letters and sounds. It is a process of recognizing patterns that are suggested by language patterns and meanings that are suggested by those patterns and using graphic cues to identify specific words. These activities occur very quickly and interactively in the brain as the reader is moving through print.

5. Reading can be an *imprecise* process. That is to say, reading is a process of predicting and confirming. It is not completely and absolutely precise. Sometimes readers predict different words, or different meanings than the author had in mind. That's natural and it happens for very logical reasons. The key is whether the reader recognizes when miscues have been made that distort meaning and self-corrects appropriately to ensure that the result of reading "works" for the reader and meets her needs.

6. Two key factors related to success in reading are not related specifically to formal reading instruction. A rich background of experience and a fluent grasp of language form the crucible in which encounters with print can be turned into meaningful experiences that can bring practical success, broadened consciousness, and deep enjoyment.

7. Writing and reading go together. Doing lots of writing complements reading by providing increased practice in letter and word recognition, exploring sound-symbol relationships, and constructing meaningful sentences.

These ideas about reading may raise questions. Let's deal with some issues that might have come up in your mind at this point:

1. You might say … "I'm a little bothered by the 'interactive' idea of reading. If a child is supposed to use all these different cueing systems together, that seems like an awful lot to expect. Doesn't that make reading harder?"

A good question. On the surface, it does seem like we're making reading unnecessarily complex, doesn't it? But what we're really doing is simply describing what good readers actually <u>do</u>. To be sure, it *is* complex. It requires explicit instruction regarding phonic decoding, a rich base of experience and knowledge, and a powerful grasp of language. When these things are present, readers naturally use these skills together. We all do. It's what we do with all things we come in contact with—we make sense of them.

Using different cues interactively actually *enhances* the likelihood of recognizing words and making meaning. We tend not to think about and appreciate what the human brain is capable of. Our brains thrive on making connections between cues and recognizing patterns in those cues. So, in promoting the interactive use of multiple cues to words and meanings, we can make reading more powerful, and more efficient.

2. You might ask … "So how do we encourage the interactive use of multiple cues when reading?"

We discussed this earlier. If the child is highly interested and motivated and engaged, we probably don't have to encourage her. In fact, attempts to help will most likely be unwelcome interruptions. On the other hand, if she happens to be struggling over a word and seems to want help, give it naturally and in a way that supports and encourages her to "see if she can figure it out." For example, you might ask, "What do you *think* the word is?"

And then, depending on the situation, you might follow up with "What makes you think that? How did you figure that out?" Or "What's the first sound?" or "Does it look like any word you know?"

The point is that by talking with the child about how she is figuring things out, you are encouraging her to engage her sense of language flow, context, and letter sounds to make predictions, and explain her reasoning. Practice in this process is what is needed to give the child a sense of independence and power in reading. Such interaction can make it something of a game that becomes a fun challenge. Children need to know they are free to use a variety of strategies to figure out print. The more they do it, the better they become at it, and the more efficient their reading becomes. Be sensitive and give the most appropriate help. The key to deciding what is appropriate is that it should help the child keep *reading for meaning*.

The bottom line is that you help a child most when you offer help that (1) promotes the goal of reading for meaning, (2) encourages the child to try his own strategies, and (3) is quick and doesn't distract him or interrupt the flow of reading.

3. You might ask ... "Isn't this like encouraging guessing?"

A logical question. Let's look at this a little. In a sense, I suppose you could say you are encouraging "guessing," though I'd prefer to use the word "predicting." When we do this, we are saying to the child, "Use what you know about meaning and language to come up with a good prediction about what that word is." By encouraging a child as discussed just above we are really saying, "You have lots of power to do this on your own. Go for it. I'll help you if you need it." By following up with these kinds of prompts, we are not promoting guessing, but rather we are promoting *focused thinking*. And, if he doesn't come up with the word quickly, tell him. Remember, the goal is to *keep on reading*. As we said, there will be plenty of opportunities to encounter the word again.

Think of it this way: What are you telling a child if you say he can't "guess?" If he can't try something and take a risk? First, you are implying that there is only <u>one right way</u> to succeed, and if he hasn't yet mastered it, he'll just have to wait till he "learns how to do it."

Second, and most important, you are implying that his efforts are not worthy, that you don't trust him to try, because you won't *let* him try. And, finally, you are implying that reading is somehow not like everything else. We learn by trying, by seeing what works, and then trying again. It's the same with reading. This, I believe, is a key idea. We want to encourage children to take risks and *try*.

4. You might ask ... "What about words that are <u>not</u> in the child's listening-speaking vocabulary?

I'm glad you asked. I told you earlier that we would get to this. There are several points to be made. First, if the book a child is reading contains a high percentage of words that are not in his listening-speaking vocabulary ... maybe you have the wrong book! If the words in the book, and the concepts which they represent, are not a part of the child's background, he can't read the book successfully *even if he is somehow able to pronounce the words correctly*. Does this mean there should be NO words that are not familiar in speech and hearing? No, but percentage of such words should be relatively low, especially when children are in the early stages of learning to read. As they become more proficient, they should be exposed to materials with more challenging vocabulary that may be new to them.

But let's go a little further. What happens when a reader does encounter a word that is not in his listening-speaking vocabulary? It depends. If pronunciation is not important, he may skip or ignore the word. (For example, when you come to a scientific term or a foreign name when you're reading, how much time do you spend tracking down the exact pronunciation?— be honest!) Or he may make an attempt to pronounce the word.

If he is reading with the intent of making meaning he will probably, at the very least, assign some meaning to the word. Often, it doesn't really matter if he pronounces the word correctly—unless he needs to use it in oral language. Let me illustrate with a personal example.

I grew up in a small town in Kansas. One day, when I was ten or eleven, I went to the local drug store, took a seat on a stool at the soda fountain, ordered my usual lemon Coke, and informed the high school girl behind the counter that I was meeting my buddy Steve and rather proudly announced that we were going to have a "wren – dez – vooze" (That's the way I pronounced it.) The young lady smiled and giggled. She then left the soda fountain and went to the back of the store and whispered something to the pharmacist, who peered over the shelves at me and also smiled. I knew something was wrong and they were laughing at me! But it wasn't until much later, when I heard someone actually say the word "rendezvous" that I realized *why* they were laughing at me.

It was one of those memorably embarrassing moments. But it also illustrates an important point. I had read that word somewhere, and I knew exactly what it meant. I didn't know that it was a French word that has been incorporated into American English with its French pronunciation. In fact, I really didn't *need* to know how it was pronounced—*until I used it in speech*! And, furthermore, the only way I would ever know how it was pronounced was to *hear* someone else pronounce it. I could never have determined the pronunciation from reading the word.

The point again is that we mostly learn how to pronounce words by *hearing* them pronounced, not by reading them. That's why we have stressed repeatedly, the child who has a rich language background has a leg up when it comes to reading.

5. You might say … "I'm a little bothered by the fact that you say reading is not a "precise" process. Shouldn't we expect children to learn to read in an exact, correct way?"

I suppose it might make us feel better if we thought we could somehow teach every child to read absolutely "correctly" all the time. But the plain truth is that reading doesn't work that way. Remember that the goal in this book is to understand how the reading process works, and based on that understanding, see how to help children become effective readers. The fact is that we all read this way. We all make miscues while reading. Some we recognize, some we don't. Some we correct. Some we don't. We are focused on the process of constructing meaning. Sometimes our need or reason for reading demands a very high degree of precision. Other times it does not. The fact that reading is not always precise is neither good nor bad. That's just the way it is.

I hope this summary and discussion has pulled together some basic ideas about how reading happens and has allowed you to get a better handle on what is happening when a child is learning how to recognize words in print.

So What?

Think about these points about reading with *your own child* in mind. Can you see these ideas applying to your child's approach to reading? How does this help you in working with your child?

What's Next?

We're coming to the final part of the book. In Chapter Twelve, I'd like to describe what it looks like when the home creates a "culture of literacy" for the children who live there.

This idea pulls together what this book is all about.

PART FOUR:
MOVING AHEAD

In Part Three of the book, we spent our time going deeper into the process that children go through in learning how to identify words in print. We have tried to help you as a parent or significant adult in a child's life to gain a clear understanding of what reading is all about and how learning to read happens. I hope that now you are confident that you understand that process better and feel more comfortable coming alongside children as they work their way toward the goal of recognizing words quickly and efficiently. It is a fascinating story, and it is amazing to see it happen right before our eyes. In this final part of the book, we are going to pull together what we have said about the role of the home in developing reading and consider some of the implications for moving ahead.

CHAPTER TWELVE:
CREATING A CULTURE OF LITERACY IN THE HOME

"Books train your mind to imagination to think big."
—Taylor Swift

We have spent lots of time trying to understand what It's like for children to make the journey from knowing nothing about reading to becoming experts at dealing with print. I have argued that what happens in the home has a fundamental role to play in that process. Navigating the effects of a major pandemic has shown even more how crucial the home is in supporting our children's grasp of essential literacy skills and knowledge.

How does that role play out? I believe it happens when we as parents and significant others in our children's lives create a *culture of literacy* in the home. In this chapter we will take some time to describe what that looks like. We will pull together lots of ideas that have been presented in earlier chapters and present a picture of developing literacy in the home that will serve to guide your thinking as you work with your own children.

What does a culture of literacy in the home look like? Essentially, it means that all the elements of literate behavior are *modeled* before children. All aspects of using print are continuously *practiced* as a part of every-day life, with the implicit understanding that the children are *expected to participate* fully. A culture of literacy means that the home is a place where language in all its forms is freely and *robustly engaged* in, where everyone's language is *valued and respected*, where mistakes are *tolerated,* where the emphasis is always on *meaning,* and where there is a pervasive *expectation of success.* A culture of literacy in the home means that printed language is used energetically—in all its forms, at all times, by *all family members*—to pursue meaning in and for the lives of all in the family.

It's a culture in which parents are reading to, with, and for their children, and parents are writing to, with, and for their children. When such a culture exists in the home, children are naturally given the tools and the dispositions that will help them become effective in dealing with print because *that's what is happening in their world.* Let's examine some aspects of a culture of literacy in the home.

A Culture of Meaning

If children are going to become skilled in using print (reading and writing), they need to have something to read and write *about.* Building a culture of literacy in the home rests on a strong foundation of experiences that are shared, giving children a rich treasure of meanings to talk about, and write about, and read about. We have been stressing this idea throughout the book. Reading to and for and with children in the home not only demonstrates how reading works, but also supplies children with a continuous fund of new ideas and understandings which then become a part of their own experience background.

A Culture of Language

We have noted that one of the things that is important for children in recognizing printed words is that they *already know* the words and how they are pronounced. The words they encounter in print are typically words they already use themselves. They have heard and have said these words hundreds of times. This is important, because if they already know words and how they are pronounced, it usually takes only a minimum of cues to recognize that a word they see on the page is a word they *already know.*

The question is, how do they know all these words? That is, of course, where the home culture comes in. The home is the place where language is learned. If the home is a place where people are engaging in language all the time, using all kinds of words, the child will have a distinct advantage when encountering print because those are words he knows! For most children, the home is the primary source of such word power. Make your home a culture of words and language.

We have also noted that another important cue to identifying printed words comes from the *flow of language* in which the words are found, or the structure of the sentences in the printed piece. Children who are used to hearing and using all kinds of sentences have a far better chance of predicting words in print.

So, make your home a place where children hear adults using all kinds of words and all kinds of sentences, especially in direct conversation. Include children in those conversations. *Expect* them to process adult language and to respond with grownup language of their own. Don't talk down to them. Let them experience all kinds of language patterns and construct all kinds of language patterns. A culture of vibrant language in the home is a powerful asset for children as they encounter language in print.

A Culture of Print

We communicate the importance of print to our children by the *presence* of print in our lives and our *involvement* with print. If our home is a place where print is *prominent* (lots of books, magazines, and documents), and a place where print is *being used* all the time (reading, writing notes and letters, using reference materials, etc.) what does that say to our children?

And what if our children, from the beginning, realized that *their* words could be put into print? What if the adults in their lives allowed and encouraged them to write what they are thinking, even though their "writing" is far from perfect? What if those around them helped them to label things in their world and to send messages to family members? In other words, what if their home was a place where putting language into print is a natural part of everyday life?

Just like oral language and reading, learning to write is a long-term developmental process that occurs best within a natural interactive social context. And, just like oral language and reading, learning to write is most likely to occur when writing is continuously modeled, when "mistakes" are tolerated, when the emphasis is placed on meaning, and there is a pervasive expectation that the child will be successful. These are the things that establish a "culture of print" in the home.

A Culture of Expectation

Children who are immersed in such a culture of print regard using print as expected and normal. This is a great gift we can give them. When children see their parents continually engaged in deep conversations, continually engaged in reading in all kinds of situations and for all kinds of reasons, continually engaged in writing in all kinds of circumstances, what do the children conclude? They conclude that reading and writing are "what happens" in the world. They come to understand that reading and writing are not only essential elements of making the world work but also are sources of great power and great joy to those in the family.

Many children become very effective readers before they start school. They become readers without a great deal of formal instruction. How does that happen? It often happens when children grow up in a home where reading and writing are a natural and integral part of everything that happens in the home.

Put briefly, when literate behavior is modeled, and the powerful results of literate behavior are consistently evident in the lives of a family, the child learns implicitly that literate behavior is the way life is lived, and that literate behavior is the *expectation* and the *norm* for life. This is a powerful message, and perhaps the most important thing that parents can provide for their children.

A Culture of Acceptance and Celebration

Finally, a culture of literacy in the home shows children that all of their attempts to make use of print are acceptable and prized. Wherever he is developmentally, the child's efforts to interact with print are acknowledged as natural, important, and meaningful. In other words, there is never a time when the child does not feel like a legitimate member of the literate community. Conferring such status on the child lays a foundation of security on which she can freely engage with all kinds of reading and writing activities with confidence and joy.

It is interesting to compare this culture of literacy in the home with the culture of reading instruction in the school. For a variety of reasons, schools do not have all the opportunities that are available to parents. Yet, at the same time, schools are held accountable for producing strong literacy performance in children. This presents a tremendous challenge for schools, which we will briefly discuss in our next chapter.

So What? – A Literate Culture Survey

Take some time to think about your home as a literate culture. Would you answer "True" or False" (or somewhere in between) for these statements?

1. There is lots of time spent in conversation with the child(ren) in our home, using all kinds of words and sentences to talk about things that are important in their life.

2. Our home is a "print-rich" environment where printed language is found abundantly and used often.

3. Lots of time is spent reading to, reading with, and reading for the children in our home.

4. Lots of time is spent writing to, writing with, and writing for the children in our home..

5. In our home, reading and writing are <u>modeled</u> all the time. My children see reading and writing as a naturally significant part of our life as a family.

CHAPTER THIRTEEN:
CHALLENGES
AND OPPORTUNITIES

"To learn to read is to light a fire."
–Victor Hugo, *Les Misérables*

One of the central things I have tried to do in this book is to make the case that the literacy environment in which a child grows up has a major impact on that child's ability and propensity to become a good reader. I have argued that a large part of what makes up good reading is rooted in the experiences and language that surround the child in his home and community environment by providing *reasons* to read, *opportunities* to read, and *tools* to read (Chapter 1).

And a major premise of this book is very simply that a thorough understanding of the reading process in its overall cultural context will enable, and indeed will entice, adults to "do the right thing" when it comes to helping children become powerfully literate (Chapter 2).

In other words, I believe that children who are immersed in the kind of literate culture that is described in this book will have a significant advantage in terms of learning to read with skill and power. Regardless of the circumstances under which reading is taught in school, a child who experiences a supportive environment that recognizes, expects, and celebrates his natural ability to develop habits of literacy will find reading instruction more accessible and reading performance more satisfying.

That said, we must recognize that it's not all so simple as it sounds. The fact is that in many homes today there are serious challenges to the emergence of strong literacy skills among children. In this chapter, we will address some of these challenges.

The Challenge of Individuality

Some might assume while reading this book that if a family supports literacy development for children in the ways that have been described, those children will inevitably become highly skilled and avid readers. I suspect that you realize this is not necessarily the case. The challenge of individuality concerns the basic notion that every child is different in a variety of ways. As a result, not all children respond the same way to a given set of circumstances.

As mentioned earlier, one of my children was an "early reader." He began long before kindergarten to predict words, to savor being read to, to "read along," to "write stories," and to eagerly jump into all sorts of interactions with print all around him. For whatever reasons, you couldn't keep him from language and print. I guess it would be nice if I could say that it was all because his mother and I were such good parents, and I am such a wise educator. Nice, but not accurate. I do believe that his mother and I "did the right thing" for the most part in raising him. But his tendency early on to invest in print was no doubt related to a variety of factors that simply "came with the package"—factors that were "built in" to a large degree in his mental and psychological foundations, including above average intelligence, a lively curiosity, a propensity for play and experimentation of all kinds, especially word play, and an eagerness to take risks and "try things out."

His sister, who was raised in exactly the same environment, with the same exposure to print and the same encounters with life experiences, was not an early reader. For her, learning to read took more time and effort. She tended to be more cautious, less adventurous, and more channeled in her interests and desires. For whatever reasons, there were clear differences between these two in their path to literacy learning. Such differences are inevitable, as any parent can attest. There are differences in innate ability, differences in learning styles and modes, differences in attention levels and interests, and differences in how children apprehend and appreciate various experiences to which they are exposed.

Because of these differences, "doing the right thing" as we have described it in this book doesn't necessarily *guarantee* the same level of literacy development for every child. Yet, **doing the right thing is still important**. It's important because it lets children know that they belong to a literate society and helps them learn to be a part of that society at whatever level of participation they choose. And, in the process, they will be immersed in valuable experiences and included in exploring those experiences through language.

Regardless of each child's unique profile in terms of interests, motivation, and abilities, doing the right thing will help to equip that child with tools that will enhance his chances for success in school and in life. We owe this to all children. It should be part of their natural environment. We owe it to each other. It helps our children become productive and engaged citizens. Each will develop in his or her own way, but doing the right thing is good for all.

The Challenge of Intentionality

What does the word, "Duh!" bring to mind? (Include a forehead slap if you like, just for emphasis.) This is that "Aha" moment when you realize that you could have, or should have, done something, but you were just not thinking about it at the time. Then you realize it – too late. Duh!

We are all busy. A myriad of things attract (or demand) our attention practically every moment of the day (and night). It's so easy to become involved in always doing the "needed" thing without thinking about doing the "right" thing. So, if we want to do the right thing with our children with regard to literacy development, we have to be *intentional* about it. This is an idea that we have emphasized often. Throughout this book, we have cited examples of ways that parents and other adults can impact a child's access to literacy skills. Typically, these are things that are not difficult and don't require special equipment or materials. What they do require is just a little bit of time and thoughtful intentional planning.

Here are some examples. Many of these ideas have been mentioned before in our discussion of understanding reading. These are just examples. If you think about it, you can come up with many more and better ideas that are clever and fun for your children. As you read through the list, adapt these ideas as age appropriate for your own children. And for each one, take a moment to think about these questions: (1) Is this something you would have naturally done without thinking about it, or is this something that you would not have done if you hadn't taken the time in advance to intentionally *decide* to do it? (2) When you take the time and effort to do this, what are you **saying** to the child about himself or herself as a reader?"

- You are getting ready to go to the grocery store. You take some time in advance to have your child write out the shopping list as you dictate it to her. You have her check off items as you pick them up, and to try to read the necessary information on the labels regarding type, size, weight, etc. of items. (What is this saying to the child?)

- You will be taking a family vacation. In advance, you find a book that takes place in the location you are going to and read to the children. You write some key words about the destination on cards and pin them to a bulletin board. You talk about them in the days and weeks before the trip. Together with the children, you look up facts about some attractions they will visit. The list could go on and on.

- Your six-year-old son has received a birthday card and gift from Aunt Suzie. Instead of a quick call or face time with Aunt Susie on the cell phone, you take the time to have him *dictate a letter* to Aunt Suzie – or write it himself with your help. He addresses the envelope, puts on a stamp, and puts it in the mailbox.

- At least one day a week, you set aside half an hour, turn off all phones and devices, grab your favorite book, have your child grab his/her favorite book, and spend the time in a pleasant place that is quiet and free from interruption. (And, of course, if and when it's appropriate, engage in some conversation about what each of you is reading.)

- If your child is reading a particular book and seems to be enjoying it, take the time to look up the author. Seek out some other books by that author, or some other books dealing with the same topic (or location, or time frame). Suggest these other books to your child.

- You are on a car trip that will take some time. As a break from children playing individually on phones or electronic tablets, play a word game. It could be seeing who is first to find and identify words beginning with each letter in the alphabet on roadside signs, or any kind of word game.

- Every once in a while, pick out a "new" word to use around your children (a word you think they don't have in their vocabulary). Use the new word on purpose in conversation with them. See if the children catch on to what it means and use it themselves when they are speaking. You might put it on a card on the bulletin board so they can see it and be reminded to use it when appropriate.

- Occasionally pick out a phrase or figure of speech that comes up in conversation and track down where it came from. For example, do you know why we say, "sleep tight"? Look it up and talk about how interesting our language is.

- Write personal notes and letters to children. (You might even mail them at the Post Office.) Let the children know that you would love to get letters from them as well.

- Take time to play lots of word games, both formal games and games you invent on the spot (like finding rhyming words, making up strings of alliterations, etc.)

- Take time to share something you learned from something you read.

- Have your child read a recipe to you as you are cooking.

Well, you get the point. We could develop an endless list of such things. But here is the key point. They won't just "happen" all by themselves. You must *make* them happen. There are opportunities every day to provide children *reasons* to read, *opportunities* to read, and to help them use the *tools* of reading. Remember, reading will happen when these three things are present together. But these things don't happen by themselves. That's where adults *must* come in. Only significant adults in a child's life can supply these three critical essentials. We have such great opportunities all the time! We must *decide* to do it. We have to be intentional.

The Challenge of Technology

The world in which my children grew up is not the world of today. And the world of tomorrow will also be different in ways that we cannot at this moment anticipate. Things are in a continual state of change, and the pace of change will continue to accelerate. These are facts that we simply must count as part of our reality. Driven largely by the almost frenetic and ubiquitous advance of technology, the way we do practically everything will continue to change dramatically in the lifetime of our children.

What will happen to reading? Will reading become "obsolete" or unnecessary? How will reading and literacy change during our children's lives? I don't have answers to these questions, and I have no ability or desire to prophesy on such matters. I do, however, think that it is necessary to pause and think about the current role of technology in relation to literacy as we have discussed it in this book. I believe that part of "doing the right thing" is trying to understand how technology has the potential to affect the development of literacy in our children.

Clearly, technology has great potential to enhance the quality, effectiveness, and efficiency of our use of information that is encoded in print. Almost every day, new methods of data collection, data usage and storage are being introduced, and new "apps" are connecting anyone with a smart phone to vast storehouses of printed materials. Once again, it's necessary to take some time to think about how the use of technology can influence children's *reasons* for reading, their *opportunities* for reading, and enhance their *tools* for reading.

The availability of technology can be helpful in relation to all three of these elements of reading development, but, at the same time, it can also be problematic. Once again, we need to be thoughtful and intentional about how we utilize technology with our children.

There may be many *reasons* for reading. For example, when it comes to reading for information, some technology applications provide immediate access to simplified information and often generate quick, simple answers, almost suggesting that deep and thoughtful reading is inappropriate or unnecessary. On the other hand, well-constructed applications can, in the process of their use, prompt readers to examine other sources or dig deeper into the body of information being examined. On the whole, technology is a great asset in the pursuit of information in print, but the motivation and reason for reading must still be in the reader. Children need someone alongside them, guiding them to find the most significant way to utilize technology to meet their needs.

In terms of reading for pleasure and enjoyment, technology can present a challenge in that the powerful pull of media action in most technology applications competes for attention. Children may find it much more compelling to compete in an action game than to read a book. At the same time, some applications designed to promote reading for pleasure provide appealing technology touches that make the reading of a book on an e-device much more appealing than reading from a book.

The bottom line is that there needs to be a good <u>reason</u> for reading— whether you are using print materials or electronic devices. We need to be careful to help children see the value of time spent in deep and reflective digestion of print, whether it's done with a book or a tablet or other device. Technology itself does not generate the reason for reading. But technology can both distract a child from reading or prompt a child to read. The emergence of technology brings a new challenge to us – we need to learn more about the technology our children are using and guide them to use that technology for the right reasons.

In terms of providing *opportunity* to read, technology can likewise be a very helpful ally in promoting reading development, or it can be a distraction that robs children of the time they might spend with print. On the one hand, because technology presents almost unlimited, instantaneous access to all kinds of printed materials, it greatly expands a child's opportunity to engage in reading about things that he needs to know or is simply interested in. On the other hand, the pull of social media and gaming applications can occupy a child for immense periods of time. Reading takes time, and time spent in the act of processing print is a critical and precious element of overall reading development. What if more of those hours spent online were spent in continuous reading?

Does technology help children acquire the *tools* of reading? The answer is probably yes and no. There is no doubt that navigating the universe of printed material available through technology gives children practice in performing many aspects of the reading act. And there are programs delivered through technology that are specifically designed to teach and practice important reading skills. At the same time, it appears likely that some aspects of online life, especially engagement with social media, and the fast-emerging development of artificial intelligence (AI) will affect reading and writing development in ways as yet unknown.

No doubt we are in the early stages of really understanding how the use of technology intersects with reading performance. Much research needs to take place to examine this relationship, and it is not our goal to examine that issue in this book. Rather, our goal is to draw attention to the challenge that technology presents, and to encourage the wise use of technology in the light of an understanding of the reading process. Once again, knowing what we now know about what reading is and how it happens, how can we "do the right thing" in terms of steering our children to use the tools of technology wisely and well?

The Challenge of Access

I hope the ideas presented in this book and the concept of creating a literate environment in the home will resonate with readers, and many children will be inspired and encouraged on their journey to becoming readers as a result. However, it's clear that in many families, there are significant elements of daily life that make the creation of such an environment very difficult.

Families that live in low-income or poverty conditions typically have less access to a wide variety of experiences for their children. In such homes, the focus of life often is simply making it through each day, and there is little time or opportunity to go beyond meeting immediate needs. This limits the range of enriching experiences that children have. It narrows the range of vocabulary used and limits the amount of verbal interaction. It has been speculated that children growing up in upper income homes may experience up to several million more language utterances than children growing up in low-income homes.

The same kind of limitations to access might be true of single-parent families, and others who have, for whatever reason, limited access to literacy experiences and materials. Even in such environments, it is still possible to take advantage of opportunities to engage children with print. Many of the suggestions we have made to "do the right thing" can happen in any home environment. But it is clearly a more challenging task in some home settings.

This is a place where *community* becomes important by working to provide a range of rich and engaging experiences for all families. School communities, church communities, neighborhood communities, and local town communities can provide opportunities to engage families in activities that include children and promote all kinds of participation in literate activities. May we all, as members of our community, work together to see that all families have access to the kinds of experiences and relationships that invite all children to experience the power and the joy of reading, and to let them know that they *belong* in the literate world.

The Challenge Facing Schools

As we have been exploring how reading happens and the ways in which children become literate, you may have found yourself thinking about your own experiences with reading instruction in school or in your child's school. If you have, you may have wondered how all the things we have been saying about the reading process fit with how reading is taught in school. It is a fascinating and important question.

Though several chapters could be devoted to describing and analyzing what happens in school reading programs, that is not the goal of this book. What I would like to do, however, is help us understand why the notion of creating a literate environment in the home is so important as a support and complement to what happens in reading instruction in school.

It is my firm belief that our teachers would love to be able to operate their classrooms in ways we have outlined when we talk about developing a "literate culture" in the home. I believe that teachers long for the kind of engagement with reading that we have described as needing to be embedded in the lives of the children they teach.

But that is not easy in a classroom setting. Think about it:

- The teacher must deal with a *variety of children*. The classroom may contain 20 (or more) children. They may come from different backgrounds, with different life experiences, different social habits, and possibly with different language preferences, as well as lots of other differences among them. In your home, you can focus, because you know your own children thoroughly and you understand deeply what each child brings to the table. This is often not the case in the classroom.

- The teacher has *limited time*. The school day is crowded with a variety of required activities, with reading instruction being only one of many areas to be attended to. In your home, time is something you have some control over. Admittedly, life at home these days is busy. But the activities we have discussed in this book can take place naturally as life at home is happening. This is not the case in the classroom.

- The teacher has *limited resources*. Aside from the materials that make up the reading curriculum used in the school, the teacher may not have resources to provide the rich array of literacy experiences and engagement we have discussed in this book. In your home, giving children all kinds of experiences and opportunities to engage with print can happen naturally. These resources and opportunities may be limited in the classroom.

- The teacher must respond to the *demand for accountability*. Schools are called on to demonstrate performance according to standards set by the state. The common response to this situation is a heavy emphasis on *testing* in order to determine if students are performing adequately. It is widely acknowledged that test scores in reading (and math) are not what they should be. And this weakness has been amplified by the learning loss that has resulted from the Covid epidemic. Teachers have to spend precious time and energy focusing on specific skills and preparing students to succeed on the tests. This is a part of school life that does not exist in the home setting. As parents you are free to celebrate your child's expeditions into reading of all kinds without a focus on measuring performance.

In short, our teachers are typically faced with a high demand for measurable performance while dealing with a large group of children with limited time and limited resources. This description of some of the challenges faced in our schools is not intended to criticize our schools or diminish the critical role of public schools in the life of our nation. Rather, this should lead us to (1) an increased appreciation for our teachers' hard work, and (2) an increased dedication to support and encourage our teachers by working to build a strong culture of literacy in our homes, which is what this book has been all be about. What an amazing gift we offer to teachers, as well as to our children, when we make our home a place where reading and writing are modeled and prized as part of the heritage we leave our children.

Where Are We?

We are coming to the end of our journey. Let's see if we can pull together the essential issues that we have encountered along the way. Here is my take:

1. The development of pervasive and vibrant literacy practice among our population, especially our young, is critical to the well-being of individuals and of our society as a whole. *The stakes are high*.

2. Learning to read is not only an academic/intellectual skill to be learned in school, but it is also—and perhaps even more importantly—a social/cultural phenomenon that is modeled, nurtured, exercised, and celebrated in the child's life in the home and community. *Learning to read happens in all domains of life*.

3. Therefore, success in developing a strong literacy base in our population depends both on high-quality teaching in our schools and on adults in children's lives "doing the right thing" to support literacy development. *We are all involved*.

4. The reading act itself is a fascinating process, and one that we can understand if we take some time to look into it. When we do, we come to understand and appreciate how amazing the process of becoming literate is and how children can naturally engage in pursuing the path to literacy. *Learning to read is not a mystery*.

5. With these understandings, we can learn to "do the right things" to help our children along the path to literacy in ways that are natural, empowering, and exciting for them and for us. *We all need to do our part.*

6. There are many challenges to literacy development. Strong literacy development needs vibrant language and experience-rich family life and requires intentional attention to doing the right things for and with children. *Doing the right thing requires effort and intentionality.*

The purpose of this book has been to remind us all that we have a role to play in the development of vital literacy skills and habits in our children. The consequences of poor literacy among our people are far-reaching and ultimately result in the loss of richness in quality of life for all of us. When a significant proportion of the population does not participate in absorbing and interacting with the body of print that catalogs and reveals the story of humankind, we lose a sense of history, common identity, and a vision of wisdom about who we are and how we can celebrate life together. The stakes are high. Let's enjoy witnessing and sharing the power of literacy together with our children.

APPENDIX: LEARNING FROM MISCUES

When we were discussing how it is that children learn to recognize words in print, (Chapters 8 and 9) we noted that readers often miscall words or make "mistakes" in identifying printed words. This is often referred to as making "miscues." Miscues are not necessarily bad. Miscues happen. We all do it.

What is interesting about miscues is that they often can tell us something about how the reader is processing print. When a child comes up with a different word than the word that is printed, it may tell us something about how the child is working to figure out words. It might give some clues about what he is expecting, what he recognizes, how he makes use of language, what background experiences he possesses or may not possess, what meanings he is making, and whether his reading is making sense to him and meeting his needs. Let's look at a few examples of what I mean.

We'll examine three examples of miscues that readers might make and see what we might learn from them. These are "made up" examples for purposes of illustration. But you can find all kinds of miscues if you listen to children reading. Here's our first example:

the text says: "She put the box in the cart."

and the child reads: "She put the box in the *cat*."

What might this miscue reveal about the reader in this reading situation? What might it tell you if the reader self-corrects? What might it tell you if he doesn't self-correct? What do you think?

Well, let's make some observations about this miscue:

- The miscue looks and sounds a lot like the original word – "cat" and "cart" look a lot alike.

- This reader seems to have a pretty good sense of phonic sounds. "cat" and "cart" both have the same beginning sound and the same ending sound.

- The miscue clearly fits the sentence structure. "cat" and "cart" are both nouns, so you could expect either of them to fit in this sentence structure "in the _____."

We see that this reader is bringing some obvious strengths to his reading. He is predicting a word that looks and sounds a lot like the word in the text and "fits" the sentence structure.

At the same time, this miscue tells us that something is not right. What is it? Well, it's clear that he's not concentrating on meaning. "She put the box in the cat." doesn't make sense (unless this is a very strange box– or a very strange cat). We might wonder how or why such a thing could happen. Actually, it's not that uncommon. The reader seems to be relying almost exclusively on the sound-symbol cues and ignoring other important cues. His prediction that the word is *cat* indicates that he's concentrating heavily on pronouncing the words and doesn't appear to be paying much attention to meaning.

This happens often with emerging readers. As a child works his way through a sentence trying to pronounce in a word-by-word fashion, his attention gets so focused on pronouncing a single word that he doesn't think about meaning. Sometimes he may forget the word he just read, not to mention forgetting the meaning of the whole sentence or paragraph he is reading.

The issue of self-correction is critical. If the reader self-corrects, that's great, indicating that he is indeed following the meaning of the passage and doesn't tolerate nonsense in the interest of attempted pronunciation.

If he doesn't self-correct, it may indicate that he is so focused on coming up with a word that looks and sounds correct that he either doesn't know he's not making sense or doesn't care.

Either way, that kind of reading is non-productive. It will be interesting to see if he comes back and self-corrects when he gets into the next sentence, or if he allows this miscue to stand, indicating that reading, for him, is largely a matter of word calling, with little or no attention to making meaning.

So, you see, reading miscues can give us some clues as to what might be happening as a child is processing print. Let's look at a couple more miscues. As you do, think about the miscues and try to answer the questions about the miscue. See if you can speculate on what the miscue is telling you about the child's reading.

Here's the next one:

Text: Alan reached to turn on the vacuum switch.

Reader: Alan reached to turn on the *light* switch.

What might this miscue reveal about the reader in this reading situation? What might it tell you if the reader self-corrects? What might it tell you if she doesn't self-correct?

What do you think?

Here the reader predicts a word that makes sense in the sentence (and perhaps in the passage) but it isn't even *close* to the printed word in terms of phonic correspondence. Why might a reader do that? Several things could be happening:

- Perhaps, based on what has come before in the text, the reader *expects* a light switch to be turned on. Perhaps her sense of the anticipated action is so strong that she doesn't pay any attention to what the actual word is.

- Or perhaps she sees the word but realizes that she doesn't know how to pronounce it and is afraid to try, so she comes up with a good substitute.

- Or it could be that she probably could come up with a pretty close pronunciation of the word, but maybe "vacuum" is not a part of her experience background and so it's not a part of her meaning vocabulary, so instead of correctly pronouncing a word that makes no sense to her, she opts to substitute a word that *does* make sense.

Once again, it will be interesting to see if, as she continues to read, she stops to revisit this miscue and tries to self-correct. If the word she chose doesn't work in terms of the meaning of the story as it continues, we would hope she would reconsider, come back to the word, and attempt a better prediction. Or, if she's an efficient reader who concentrates on meaning, she may realize the miscue and adjust her thinking without coming back to repronounce the word out loud—we may never know. Clearly many things could be happening. These things are not "bad" or "good." They are simply strategies that are naturally employed by readers in the process of navigating print.

Let's look at one more miscue:

Text:	Larry ate the tacos for lunch.
Reader:	Larry ate the *tomatoes* for lunch.

What might this miscue reveal about the reader in this reading situation? What might it tell you if the reader self-corrects? What might it tell you if he doesn't self-correct? What do you think?

This is an interesting miscue. We can infer some positive speculations about the reader.

- First, the reader's miscue clearly fits the meaning of the sentence, indicating that he is most likely paying attention to meaning and so inserts a word that "makes sense."

- Second, his miscue begins with the same sound as the word in the text, hinting that he is probably paying attention to phonic characteristics of the word.

- Given these observations, we might speculate about why he chose this particular response. It's possible that he simply didn't look carefully enough at the word. However, it's also possible that he may not be familiar with tacos but does know about tomatoes. In other words, the issue could be one of background experience and vocabulary, and not about reading skill at all.

- The miscue is interesting because it illustrates how several different factors might be influencing a particular reading performance. Only when we observe a *pattern* of miscues can we begin to really draw conclusions. In addition, if the reader self-corrects, we might change our ideas about what is happening.

We've looked at only three very simple examples of miscues that children might make while reading. The range of possible miscue patterns is endless. The point is not to describe all the kinds of miscues. That would be impossible and pointless. The point is, however, that miscues <u>do</u> happen, and they can often tell us something about how the reader is processing print. Remember, miscues are not necessarily mistakes. Miscues are not random accidents. Miscues are a common part of the process of recognizing printed words. Miscues and self-correction strategies reveal a lot about how a reader is processing print.

I am not suggesting that we should always make our children read out loud. However, while they are learning, reading out loud is natural and appropriate. When we do find children reading out loud, we can observe the kinds of responses they make. This can often tell us something about how they are figuring out what words are.

ABOUT THE AUTHOR

Tom Schroeder is a retired Professor of Elementary Education at Ball State University, serving at Ball State for thirty-six years as a Professor, Department Chair, and Associate Dean. His passion for understanding how literacy develops in children began when, after graduating from the University of Kansas, he spent six years as a classroom teacher at Apache Elementary School in Overland Park, Kansas.

Encouraged by two mentors at the University of Kansas, Tom returned to KU, graduating with his PhD degree in 1973. Since that time, he has continued to ponder and examine the notion of how it is that children become readers, and what role the home, along with the school, plays in making that happen.

This book is very simply the culmination of many years of thought and study, motivated by the belief that literacy is among the most essential foundations of success for us as individuals and as a society. It is presented in the hope that it gives parents understanding, and as a result, confidence to joyfully journey along with their children as they experience the power and joy of reading.